Beginning Platino Game Engine

Abhishek Nandy
Debashree Chanda

Apress®

Beginning Platino Game Engine

Abhishek Nandy
Kolkata, West Bengal, India

Debashree Chanda
Kolkata, West Bengal, India

ISBN-13 (pbk): 978-1-4842-2483-0
DOI 10.1007/978-1-4842-2484-7

ISBN-13 (electronic): 978-1-4842-2484-7

Library of Congress Control Number: 2016959663

Managing Director: Welmoed Spahr
Lead Editor: Pramila Balan
Technical Reviewer: Sumitra Bagchi
Editorial Board: Steve Anglin, Pramila Balan, Laura Berendson, Aaron Black, Louise Corrigan, Jonathan Gennick, Robert Hutchinson, Celestin Suresh John, Nikhil Karkal, James Markham, Susan McDermott, Matthew Moodie, Natalie Pao, Gwenan Spearing
Coordinating Editor: Prachi Mehta
Copy Editor: Teresa F. Horton
Compositor: SPi Global
Indexer: SPi Global
Artist: SPi Global

Distributed to the book trade worldwide by Springer Science+Business Media New York, 233 Spring Street, 6th Floor, New York, NY 10013. Phone 1-800-SPRINGER, fax (201) 348-4505, e-mail orders-ny@springer-sbm.com, or visit www.springeronline.com. Apress Media, LLC is a California LLC and the sole member (owner) is Springer Science + Business Media Finance Inc (SSBM Finance Inc). SSBM Finance Inc is a Delaware corporation.

For information on translations, please e-mail rights@apress.com, or visit www.apress.com.

Apress and friends of ED books may be purchased in bulk for academic, corporate, or promotional use. eBook versions and licenses are also available for most titles. For more information, reference our Special Bulk Sales–eBook Licensing web page at www.apress.com/bulk-sales.

Any source code or other supplementary materials referenced by the author in this text are available to readers at www.apress.com. For detailed information about how to locate your book's source code, go to www.apress.com/source-code/. Readers can also access source code at SpringerLink in the Supplementary Material section for each chapter.

Printed on acid-free paper

This book is dedicated to my Mom and Dad. (Abhishek Nandy)

Contents at a Glance

Contents

About the Authors

Abhishek Nandy is the second individual from India to earn the prestigious Intel Black Belt Developer designation. He is also a Microsoft MVP and Intel Software Innovator.

He writes at CodeProject, and he is also a Featured Developer at the Devmesh Intel site (https://devmesh.intel.com/). He has proposed two whitepapers for Intel (RealSense with Windows UAP and Windows 10 UWP Integration). He is the founder of Geek Monkey Studios. His startup was among the top 50 at the Digital India Innovate Challenge and Intel's IoT Ultimate Coder Challenge.

He can be contacted at abhishek.nandy81@gmail.com. His YouTube Channel can be found at https://www.youtube.com/channel/UCD1IBC7l6QNpPNMYjubi0tg.

Debashree Chanda is a designer at Geek Monkey Studios. She is learning Platino and she plans to build lot of apps on it. She has also won several challenges at TopCoder. She writes at C# Corner with the profile http://www.c-sharpcorner.com/members/debashree-chanda4. She is also a premium instructor at Udemy.

About the Technical Reviewer

Sumitra Bagchi has a Masters in Computer Application and has worked in web development and software development for more than six years, working as an individual contributor for the last three years. Her current focus is on Docker, PHP7, IOT, Xamarin, and IBM Bluemix. She has won worldwide challenges through Spiceworks and she also won an award at the worldwide Flir Camera Challenge. She has also worked on Windows 365 development projects. She is a premium instructor with Udemy Online Tutorials.

Acknowledgments

I would like to acknowledge my mom, dad, my brother, and my co-author Debashree Chanda. Thanks go to the entire Intel Software Innovator Team, Intel Black Team, and Microsoft MVP community. Special thanks go to Bob Duffy who showed me the path to contribute to Intel, Ujjwal Kumar, Abhishek Narain, my friend Sourav Lahoti, and one of my fellow innovators Rupam Das, as well as the CEO of Platino, Peach Icaza Pellen, and also to the CEO of Black Gate Games, John Gould.

—Abhishek Nandy

I would like to acknowledge Peach Icaza Pellen, whom I admire the way she has become so well known in the game developer community and I would like to follow in her footsteps.

—Debashree Chanda

Foreword

About Platino

Platino is the perfect game engine for developers because it was created from the ground up by experts in app development, in engineering, in OpenGL and, critically, by people who had already shown success in creating SDKs for mobile platforms.

Two of the engineers, Carlos Icaza and Peach Icaza Pellen, were previously part of the team behind a popular SDK used, in its prime, by over 100,000 developers. They found that this SDK, although good, was not powerful enough for game developers and while great for beginner, it was far too rigid for more experienced programmers who needed more flexibility.

With those things in mind they teamed up with Kota Iguchi and other industry experts and set about making Platino easy enough for new developers but also so powerful and flexible for experienced programmers; they knew they had succeeded when in the same month a class of high school students adopted Platino for their course work, while elsewhere it was being used to develop a mobile game for Disney which went on to reach the top 10 on several stores.

Utilizing Javascript means that Platino is very easy to pick up for anyone with development experience, regardless of how familiar they are with the mobile technology; but it also grows with the developer, who can work with the engine at a high or low level depending on what is required. If a developer wants to include native code, such as Obj-C or Java, they are able to do so without any limitations.

From a single codebase, developers can then build their applications for iOS and Android, with more platforms to be added in the future.

Beginning Platino Game Engine is a book which gives an insight into Platino Game Engine. Good beginners content.

About Peach Icaza Pellen

Peach is a Platino expert, having been involved with the engine since its inception. Originally Head of Developer Relations at Ansca Mobile, where she worked with Carlos Icaza, creator of Corona SDK, she moved to Lanica when the Platino engine was created in 2012. As Senior Technical Writer, she wrote the majority of the engine's tutorials and documentation, and is well-known as the go-to community for Platino's many developers, from indies to large studios.

When not evangelizing Platino, she contributes resources to websites devoted to helping new developers learn how to create apps on a variety of platforms and works on her apps, along with contributing to applications other developers are building; she had directly worked on over 200 mobile applications and libraries of her creation are used in over 50,000 apps all around the world. As if that weren't enough, she is also a regular contributor to App Developer magazine, continuing to share her knowledge and passion for app-creation, and works closely with Intel as one of their few female investors.

Peach is now continuing her devotion to quality software and app development, directing the Platino Studio team as well as overseeing Platino Inc.'s Professional Software Consulting division.

CHAPTER 1

■ ■ ■

Introduction to the Game Engine

The game engine has become an essential part of creating a game. The game engine helps developers bring the game to life. The important aspects include audio, video rendering, camera positioning, scene creation, and use of a physics engine in a game.

Every top game company now tries to adapt its own game engine so that they can optimize it for its entire game creation. It is said a good game engine and knowledge are critical to the successful creation of a game.

We Start Here

In this book we cover the basics of game engines, then we introduce the Platino game engine. We go through the steps for installing the engine and then examine the architecture of the engine to see what it is based on. We then start developing apps on the Platino game engine. The focus then moves to creative coding and the different languages and frameworks that support it. We then move on to processing, and we see how Processing JS and also an extension of Processing named P5.js is used to build Windows 10 UWP apps. In the last section, we extend Processing for IoT using Temboo and then we conclude. The journey will be awesome!

In this first chapter we cover the following topics:

- What is a game engine?

- Making a game engine.

- How a game engine works.

- Different game engines.

- Some special HTML 5 physics libraries.

What Is a Game Engine?

Let's start this way: We are playing Prince of Persia and want to figure out how rewind works in the game. We start to see the depth of development of the game. The awesome physics in the game give us an idea of just how difficult it is to complete a game with such detailed effects. There are visuals, graphics rendering, and high-quality audio. After going through the analysis, we find that a game engine is made up of different components, as shown in Figure 1-1. A game engine is a framework for developing games based on some core areas. Let's take a closer look.

Electronic supplementary material The online version of this chapter (doi:10.1007/978-1-4842-2484-7_1) contains supplementary material, which is available to authorized users.

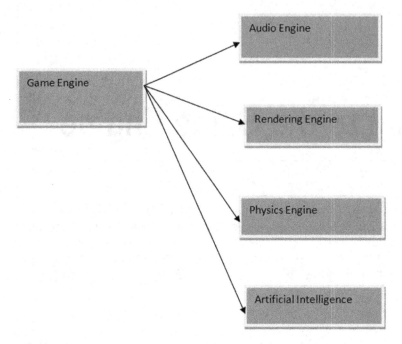

Figure 1-1. *Details of game engine components*

We next break down the terms that are important for understanding game engines.

Audio Engine

The audio engine is very important because sounds play an important role in games. If our playable character is fighting with an enemy, and the fighting mechanism is a sword, when the player makes contact with an enemy's sword we need to produce a sound effect. That work is done by the audio engine. Also, to make the ambience interesting, we add background music and sound effects.

Rendering Engine

The rendering engine helps to determine what is shown as output to users. It is a visual treat for a user when he or she is taken into a game. Rendering helps bring the graphical content of a game to life exactly the way we intended. Generally with the help of software, we get the desired effect.

Let's take a look at the mechanism (Figure 1-2). We don't want to overstress the graphics processing unit (GPU). Because at times the graphics rendered are very high quality, it requires a great deal of processing power and can result in degraded performance. Hence we add a software layer abstraction with the help of appplication programming interfaces (APIs) so that the software base does not have a direct interaction with the GPU. The final result output is shown to the users and they are able to interact accordingly. The WebGL is the new standard for rendering cool graphical user interface (GUI) effects at the browser. We describe each API next, as they hold the graphics part together.

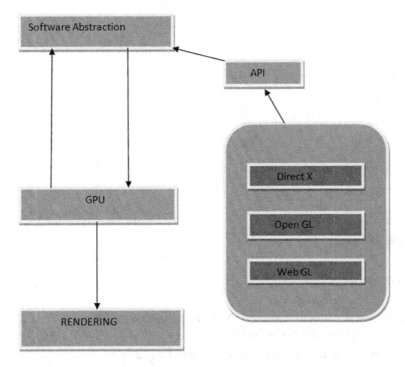

Figure 1-2. *Software abstraction over the GPU*

Direct X

Direct X (Figure 1-3; see `https://support.microsoft.com/en-in/kb/179113`) is a combination of APIs especially for handling rendering the best multimedia from the perspective of game programming on Microsoft platforms. The Microsoft Direct X Software Development Kit (SDK) allows a combination of APIs targeting it for both 32-bit and 64-bit platforms. The SDK is used to create graphic-intensive applications for Windows platforms. Direct X is a combination of APIs such as direct 3D, Direct Draw, and so on. The latest version of Direct X is Direct X 12.

Figure 1-3. *Microsoft Direct X*

Some important versions of Direct X are shown in Figure 1-4.

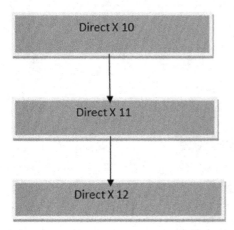

Figure 1-4. *Important versions of Direct X*

- *Direct X 10*: This version was available from Windows Vista. Backward compatibility was also maintained. It featured improved graphics rendering.

- *Direct X 11*: The major update for this version was multithreading for multicore support.

- *Direct X 12*: This version was launched alongside Windows 10. For better resolution of graphics, low-level APIs were introduced.

Open GL

Open GL (Figure 1-5; see `https://www.opengl.org/`) is a cross-platform API that helps in rendering 2D and 3D vector graphics. The most important current introduction to the Open GL standard is Vulkan. Vulkan (Figure 1-6; see `https://www.khronos.org/vulkan/`) is a next-generation OpenGL initiative. The API targets high performance with lower optimization and less pressure on the GPU or CPU for processing the rendered output.

Figure 1-5. *Open GL*

Figure 1-6. *Vulkan API for graphics*

The following are the main advantages of the Vulkan API:

- It is not restricted to a specific operating system (OS), so it can be scaled up and scaled down accordingly, including support meant for mobile OS, too, such as Tizen, Linux (Ubuntu Mobile), and so on.

- Better multicore utility.

- Low CPU overhead.

As soon as the Vulkan API was released, Intel was ready with graphics drivers for Vulkan, and over time the industry has moved toward Vulkan.

At GDC 2016, Intel shared their benchmark for Vulkan API at their booth on devices ranging from tablets to PCs, and so on. The demo showcased DOTA 2 running on Valve's source engine (see Figure 1-7), and had already started porting it using the Linux open source driver (Figure 1-8; see `https://01.org/linuxgraphics/blogs/jekstrand/2016/open-source-vulkan-drivers-intel-hardware`).

Figure 1-7. *Vulkan API running DOTA 2 using Valve's source engine*

5

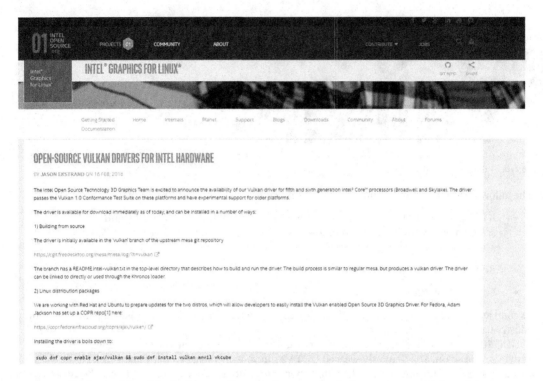

Figure 1-8. *The Intel Graphics for Linux web page where we obtain the open source Vulcan drivers*

Another internal demo was shown running on Windows. That demo showcased some of the cool features of the Vulkan API, and the frame rate obtained was around 40 frames per second (fps). The Android demo showcased the same features with nearly 30 fps.

WebGL

WebGL (Figure 1-9) is specially designed for rendering 3D graphics processing at the web browser level. It is entirely based on JavaScript. Some important WebGL libraries are Threes, D3.js, and so on.

Figure 1-9. *WebGL logo*

Physics Engine

Thinking of physics conjures up thoughts of Newton's laws of motion. These laws balance the world's activity pertaining to gravity in everyday scenarios. If we need to replicate the same condition and logic in terms of games, therefore, we have to use physics engine.

Some important physics-related aspects of game engines are the following:

- Collision detection.

- Soft body dynamics.

- Brownian motion, and so on.

One of the most important game engines is Havok's game engine, so let's take a look.

Havok Engine

The Havok engine (Figure 1-10; see `http://www.havok.com/`) is a suite of software using Havok's technology specifically targeting games. It produces life-like effects in games. Its collision detection, dynamics of rigid bodies, and physics simulation are unique and very accurate. The features of the engine are shown in Figure 1-11.

Figure 1-10. *Havok engine logo*

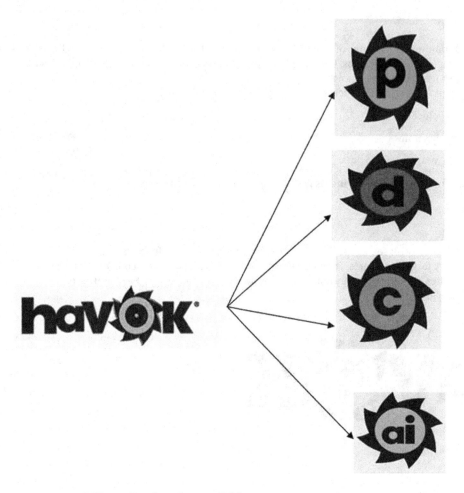

Figure 1-11. *Different Havok options available*

The different Havok engine options are as follows:

- Havok physics (P).
- Havok destruction (D).
- Havok cloth (C).
- Havok artificial intelligence (AI).

Artificial Intelligence in Games

AI plays a pivotal role in games. This logic provides building blocks for key player engagements in the game. The logic between our player character and the surroundings can be highly engaging if we implement a good AI logic.

AI is nothing but a set of algorithms implemented to get our logics implemented in a game. The A* algorithm (Figure 1-12) is one of the most popular algorithms implemented in games to help us with path finding and graph traversals.

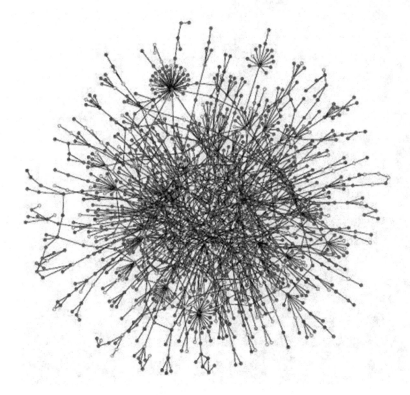

Figure 1-12. *A* algorithm depiction*

Generally in different game engines, A* algorithms helps in character tracking to a point. In the Unity game engine (which we describe briefly later on), it helps with nemeses and also proper guidance of a character to a destination.

Blend Trees in the Unity Game Engine

Blend trees in games are similar to a state automata where the machine goes through specified steps. In the Unity engine, it is the state of animations that reflect the same (see Figure 1-13).

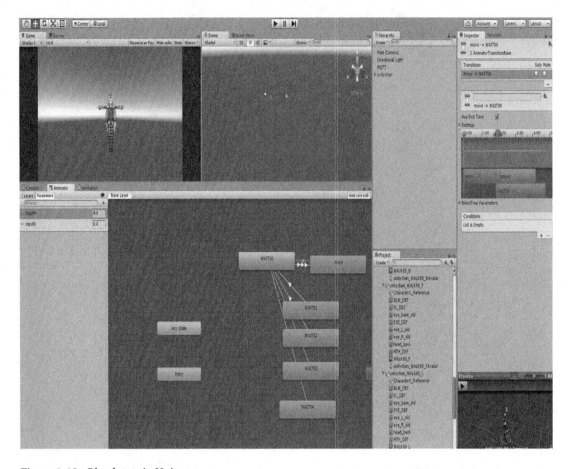

Figure 1-13. *Blend state in Unity*

Making a Game Engine

Creating a game engine of our own is a very tedious job. It requires a lot of hard work, time, energy, and brain power to get the perfect logic within which your game will work. It usually requires an input and the output. The input is the game and the output is the result, or how the game works. Creating a game engine involves several implementations of the logic defined previously with the included framework for our game environment.

Figure 1-14 shows how the development of game engine logic works.

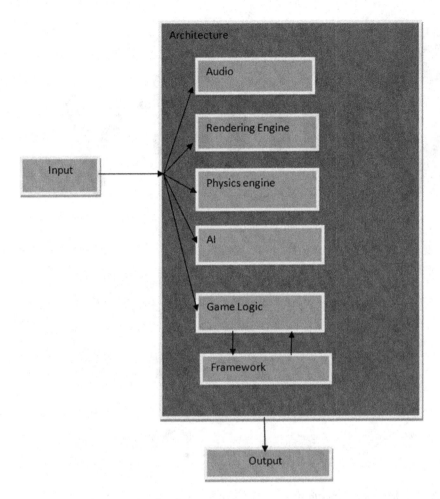

Figure 1-14. *Game engine development logic*

Different Game Engines

In this section we discuss the game engines that are available on the market and are useful for making games. These game engines will give you an idea about what is the best game engine available.

Unity Game Engine

Unity (Figure 1-15l see https://unity3d.com/) is one of the most versatile game engines being used in this industry today. It supports 21 platforms. Figure 1-16 shows the flow of Unity for some common platforms.

Figure 1-15. *Unity logo*

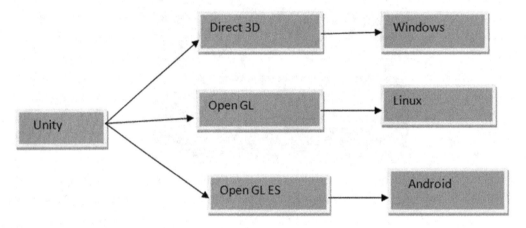

Figure 1-16. *Unity and its acceptance across platforms*

As per Figure 1-16, Unity uses Direct 3D for Windows-based application, Open GL for Linux platforms, and Open GL ES for Android applications.

Unity is full of features. The following are some of the most important ones.

- Life-like animation.
- Scripting with C#, JavaScript, or Boo.
- Unmatched import pipeline.
- Fully extensible editor.
- State machines.
- Blend trees.

- Inverse kinematics.

- Physics-based shading.

- Shuriken-based particle system.

- 2D physics.

- Sprite packer.

- Automatic sprite animation.

- Multithreaded simulation.

- Advanced vehicle physics.

Unreal 4 Game Engine

Unreal 4 (Figure 1-17; see https://www.unrealengine.com/what-is-unreal-engine-4) is a game engine developed by Epic Games. The most important part of the engine is that its scripting option is C++, which is very fast for compilations. The Unreal Development Kit and Unreal script have evolved as Blueprints in Unreal 4. Access for Unreal 4 across major platforms is shown in Figure 1-18.

Figure 1-17. *Unreal4 logo*

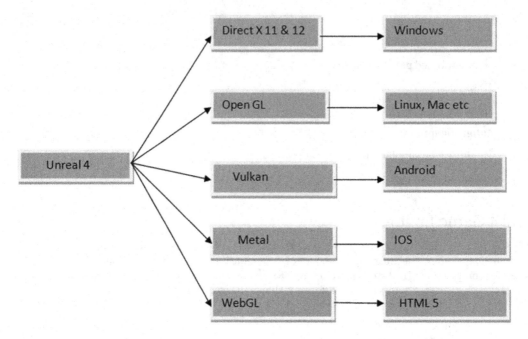

Figure 1-18. *Platform accessibility for Unreal 4*

Blueprints

Blueprints are the newly introduced visual scripting tool in Unreal 4. It is completely a node-to-node-based logic that adds the game logic to the game you are building. It supports the object-oriented paradigm. The scripting mechanism can be interlinked with C++-based programming techniques. Figure 1-19 is an example of how Blueprints look.

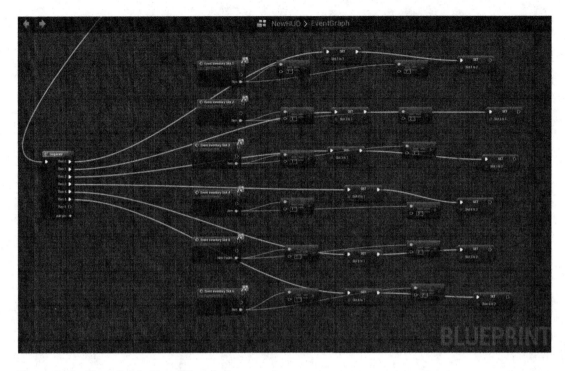

Figure 1-19. *Blueprints in Unreal 4 engine.*

Features of Unreal 4 Engine

The following are some important features of Unreal 4 engine.

- Supports advanced Direct X 11 and Direct X 12 features.
- Cascade visual effects.
- New material pipeline.
- Blueprint visual scripting.
- Live Blueprint debugging.
- Content browser.
- Persona animation.
- Matinee cinematics.
- Terrain and foliage.
- Postprocess effects.
- Simulate and immersive views.
- Instant game preview.
- Artificial intelligence.
- Audio.
- Learning middleware integration.

15

Some Special HTML5 and JavaScript Libraries

Box2D

Box2D is a physics engine that helps in simulating rigid body physics in 2D. Box2D generates continuous collision detection between objects. It is fast and easy to implement. An example is shown in Figure 1-20.

Figure 1-20. *Box2D example*

MatterJS

MatterJS (Figure 1-21; see `http://box2d.org/`) is essentially a 2D physics engine for the Web.

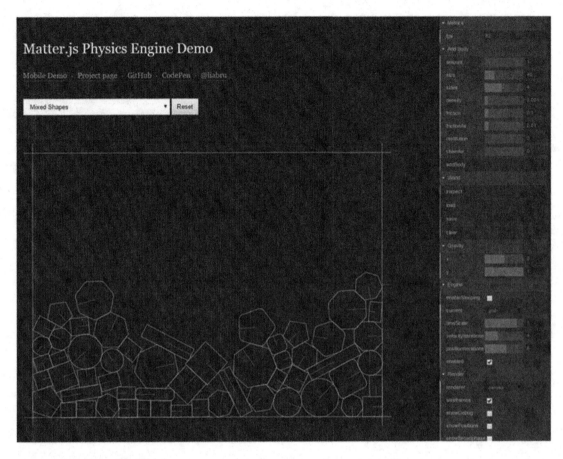

Figure 1-21. *MatterJS example*

Some important features of MatterJS are rigid body simulation, component body simulation, and much more. It helps in bringing the physics simulation into a browser-based environment.

Summary

In this chapter we have covered what game engines are, the components of a game engine, major game engines, and the physics related to game engines. This chapter gives you a basic idea of how a game engine works. We continue on to explore the future of game engines and their continuously evolving nature.

CHAPTER 2

■ ■ ■

The Platino Game Engine

In this chapter, we go through what exactly the Platino game engine does and how it has evolved. We also take a look at the people behind the game engine.

Platino Game Engine

Platino is a cross-platform game engine.The main purpose for creating the game engine was to use JavaScript to build native mobile games and apps.

The Platino Internet home page is shown in Figure 2-1.

Figure 2-1. *The Platino home page*

© Abhishek Nandy and Debashree Chanda 2016
A. Nandy and D. Chanda, *Beginning Platino Game Engine*, DOI 10.1007/978-1-4842-2484-7_2

The content in the web site is divided into three parts, shown in Figure 2-2: Download, Learn, and Build.

Figure 2-2. *The Platino page web site categories*

Download

As the name suggests, clicking the Download icon takes you to another page where you can try Platino for a 30-day trial or purchase a yearly license for $199 (see Figure 2-3).

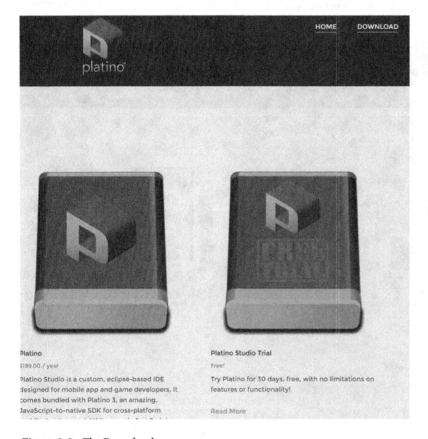

Figure 2-3. *The Download page*

Learn

The Learn section provides a lot of options (see Figure 2-4), including resources and code samples to get a grip on Platino.

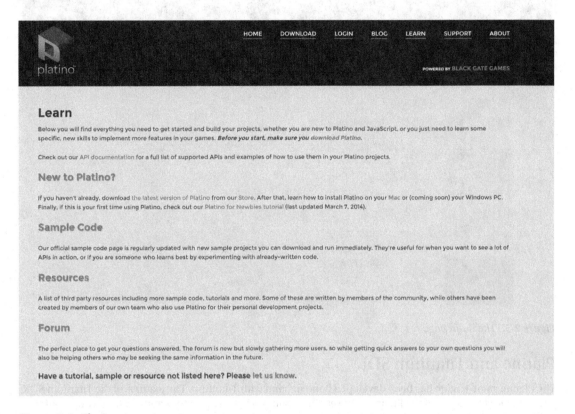

Figure 2-4. *The Learn page*

Build

In the Build section (Figure 2-5), there are plenty of samples that you can and adapt and modify to your liking.

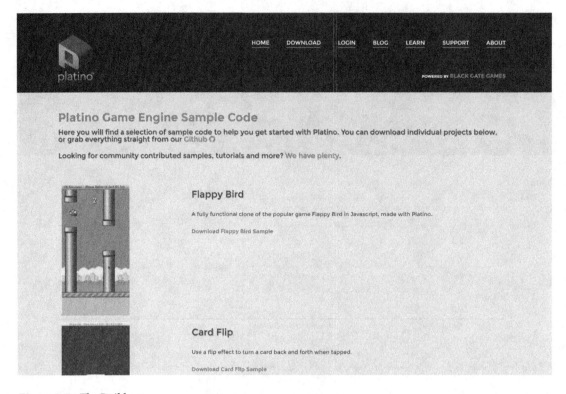

Figure 2-5. *The Build page*

Platino and Titanium SDK

The Platino game engine has been developed hand in hand with Titanium. The features of the Titanium SDK added to the capabilities of the Platino game engine result in a powerful combination to work with. Coding in Platino is done entirely using JavaScript and the result is a very robust application.

Figure 2-6. *Titanium SDK logo*

Titanium SDK

The Titanium SDK (Figure 2-6; see `http://builds.appcelerator.com/#master`) allows usage of native capability through JavaScript for iOS and Android. Titanium uses hardware-specific features such as the Android menu button. We can use OS-specific controls for iOS such as COCOA UI controls. It uses a platform-oriented notification mechanism (Figure 2-7).

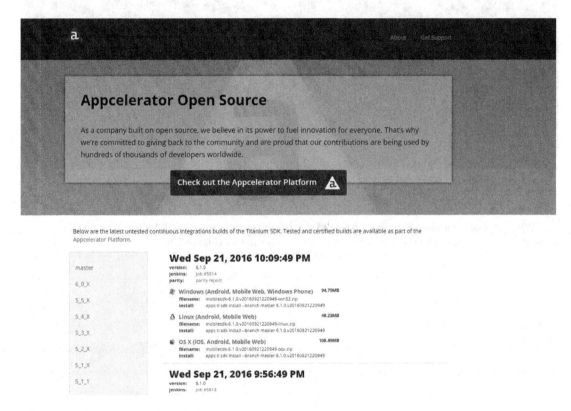

Figure 2-7. *The Titanium SDK platform*

Alloy Framework

The Alloy framework (Figure 2-8) is based on a Model View Controller architecture and has built-in support for Backbone.js as well as Underscore.js. These three combinations works perfectly with each other, so a build consisting of Titanium and Platino, and implemented over an Alloy framework template, shapes up the app very well, and it is easy to use and robust, too.

Figure 2-8. *The Alloy framework*

When we use a template from Platino Studio that involves the Titanium SDK Platino game engine capability, we can build very good looking apps. The flow is shown in Figure 2-9.

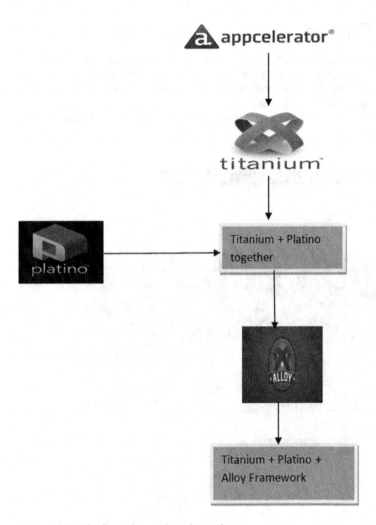

Figure 2-9. *The flow of a combined template*

How the Engine Has Evolved

The latest version of Platino game engine, release 3.0.0, has come a long way. It was originally Lanico's Platino engine and was available from the Web directly from Lanico's web site. With the recent acquisition of the Platino game engine by Black Gate Games, the entire Platino engine has been revamped and the newly available Platino engine is available from at `https://platino.io/`.

Currently the Platino game engine is powered by Black Gate Games (`http://www.blackgategames.com/`). The web site appears as shown in Figure 2-10.

Figure 2-10. *Black Gate Games web site*

Core Features of Platino Game Engine

Let's take a look at the core features of the Platino game engine.

- Because Platino uses the widely accepted Titanium SDK, we can create native games and apps using JavaScript.

- Being cross-platform, we can target different OS.

- Platino engine supports Open GL.

- It has complete Sprite Sheet support.

- It uses an isometric tile engine, producing the best effect for achieving the optimum performance of the GPU.

- Platino uses a Physics JS module to produce very realistic physics effects in games.

People Behind the Game Engine

Let's take a detailed look at people who are behind the Platino game engine.

John Gould

John Gould is the CEO of Black Gate Games, the company that now powers the Platino game engine. Gould founded Avatar Software in 2003 with the aim of becoming the premier boutique software development firm in the Nashville area. He has more than 15 years of experience developing software and managing successful projects for companies from 5 employees up to 50,000. Gould started developing mobile applications in 2010. As he saw the increasing need for outstanding mobile app developers, he cofounded Codex Labs to offer mobile development training for Appcelerator's Titanium Studio. He is immensely talented and holds the entire Black Gate Games team together.

Peach Icaza Pellen

Peach Icaza Pellen an Intel Software Innovator and CEO of Platino Game Studio. She is immensely talented and is skilled at teaching and sharing with the development community. She helps fellow developers to master concepts, participates regularly at meetups, and speaks about Platino game engine and helps others adapt to the new features of the game engine. She is a Platino expert, having been involved with the engine since its inception. Originally Head of Developer Relations at Ansca Mobile, creator of the Corona SDK, she moved to Lanica when the Platino engine was created in 2012. As a senior technical writer, she wrote the majority of the engine's tutorials and documentation, and is well-known as the go-to community contact for Platino's many licensees.

When not evangelizing Platino, Pellen found time to create Techority, a web site devoted to helping new developers learn how to create apps on a variety of platforms. If that weren't enough, she is also a regular contributor to *App Developer* magazine, continuing to share her knowledge and passion for app creation.

She is now continuing her devotion to quality software and app development, directing the Platino Studio team as well as overseeing Platino, Inc.'s Professional Software Consulting division.

Joseph Austin

Joseph Austin is a lead developer for the Platino game engine and adds stability and impetus to the game engine.

Carlos Manuel Icaza (1966–2016)

Although he is no longer with us, Carlos Manuel Icaza's willingness to help the community of developers has been always rich. He was immensely talented as an individual and he had the ability to inspire others.

He had 20 years of engineering and management experience, including managing various teams at Adobe such as the Flash Lite team, Flash Mobile Authoring, Flash Cast, and Adobe Illustrator. He was also responsible for creating and developing Adobe's entire mobile authoring strategy, now deployed across the entire Adobe Creative Suite.

Aside from managing experience, Icaza shipped leading and award-winning, industry-standard applications such as Flash Lite (deployed in over 2 billion devices), Flash Authoring, Adobe Creative Suite, Adobe Mobile Device Central, Adobe Illustrator, SVG, Adobe Pagemill, Micrografx Windows Draw, and Deneba Canvas.

In 2007 he founded and was the CEO of Ansca, Inc, which makes the Corona SDK and successfully closed a $1.5 million series a round. In 2014, he cofounded RCTSports, a wearable sensor company, providing tracking and analytics for college and professional teams and athletes to provide insights into their performance.

He successfully attended numerous meetups in the United States targeting the swift programming. A man of such knowledge and strength will be deeply missed.

Summary

In this chapter we have seen all the details of the Platino game gngine. We have given a brief introduction to it and covered details of the core features of the game engine.

CHAPTER 3

Installing and Setting Up Platino Game Engine

In Chapter 2 we had an introduction to the Platino game engine and the people behind it. This game engine is based on Titanium SDK, as we discussed. The process of integrating Platino game engine is handled via Titanium SDK, so this chapter covers how to install the Platino game engine within a Windows environment.

The Content

In this chapter we cover the dependencies and the installation process for the Platino game engine. The content of the chapter is given here.

- The Platino Store and the process of getting Platino
- Installation of the Platino game engine

The Platino Store and the Process of Getting Platino

The way to get the Platino game engine is online. The Platino game engine is available for download from the Platino Store (http:/platino.io/store).

In the store, there are two options for downloading Platino. A Platino Studio 30-day trial version has no limitations on features and functionality. The other version, of the full version of Platino, is available for $199 per year. The store looks like Figure 3-1.

© Abhishek Nandy and Debashree Chanda 2016

A. Nandy and D. Chanda, *Beginning Platino Game Engine*, DOI 10.1007/978-1-4842-2484-7_3

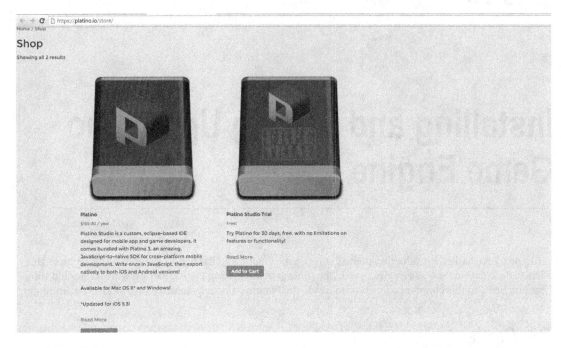

Figure 3-1. *Platino Store download options*

Make your selection and click Add to Cart. Figure 3-2 shows how the cart is updated.

Figure 3-2. *Adding a product to the cart*

Click Proceed to Checkout to move to the checkout page. There you need to fill in all the details to continue the download. The checkout page looks like Figure 3-3.

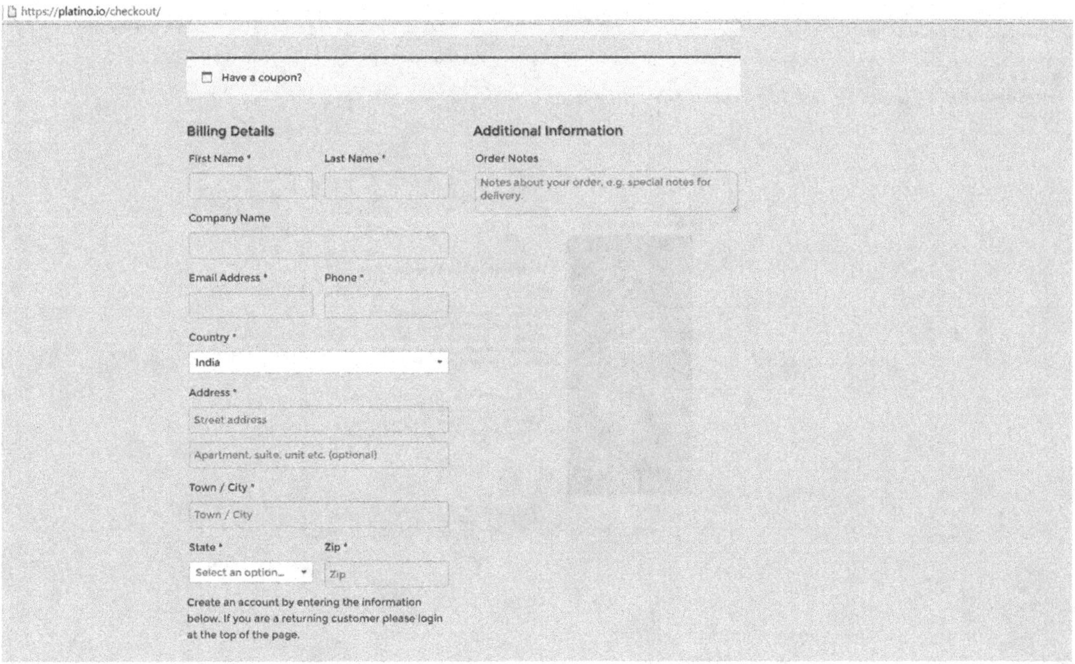

Figure 3-3. *The checkout page*

When you fill in the details and create an account, you can then place your order. The download link will then be sent to your e-mail. From the download link, choose your operating system and start your download.

Installation of Platino Game Engine

Once you downloaded the linked file, the compressed file is saved on your computer. You need to unzip it. Once you do, the installation file (Figure 3-4) is ready to be updated and installed to get you started with Platino.

Figure 3-4. *Platino Studio setup file*

Double-click the .exe file to start the installation process, then click Next to continue, as shown in Figure 3-5.

Figure 3-5. *Starting the installation process*

As the installation starts, the Platino package able to detect dependencies and prompts the user to install the dependencies. The first dependency is node.js: If it is not on your computer, it will start installing from the Web as shown in Figure 3-6. Click Next to proceed with the installation. The Node.js dependency is a very powerful and very useful open source cross-platform JavaScript runtime environment for creating tools and applications that are easy to use. Node.js uses event-driven architecture for its development and packaging, with a wonderful usage of asynchronous I/O. Node.js allows useful operation of creating web servers and networking tools using JavaScript that can handle various amounts of core functionality that evolves the architecture quickly. The installation process is shown in Figure 3-7, where the Node.js installation wizard starts.

Figure 3-6. *Installing the first dependency*

Figure 3-7. *The process of installation continues*

The Node.js Setup Wizard continues on its own. Just click Next as shown in Figure 3-8.

Figure 3-8. *Continuing the Node.js installation*

The setup configures the path and adds the details of Node.js to the environment variable. The path configuration and all the steps for a custom setup are shown in Figure 3-9.

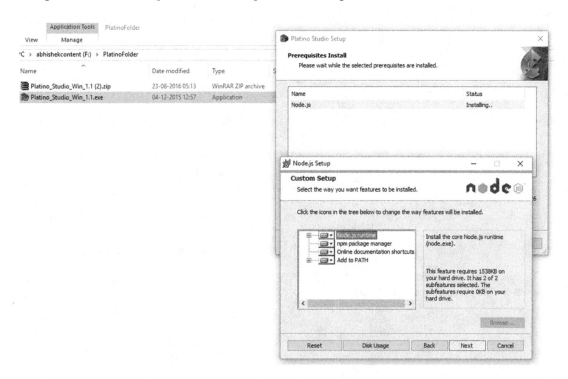

Figure 3-9. *The setup configures the path of Node.js*

In the next step, shown in Figure 3-10, we see that the setup for Node.js is complete, and the other dependencies for Paltino are installed next.

Figure 3-10. *Node.js installation complete*

The next step works on getting the configuration scripts ready. You will see a console window or command prompt (see Figure 3-11) that will guide you through the steps.

Figure 3-11. *Command prompt starts its scripting process*

In the next step the command prompt installs the Titanium SDK and also configures the setup for installing the Alloy framework, which is necessary for getting the Platino game engine installed. Figure 3-12 shows you this step.

Figure 3-12. *Installing Titanium SDK*

The next step installs the dependencies of Titanium SDK step by step, as shown in Figure 3-13.

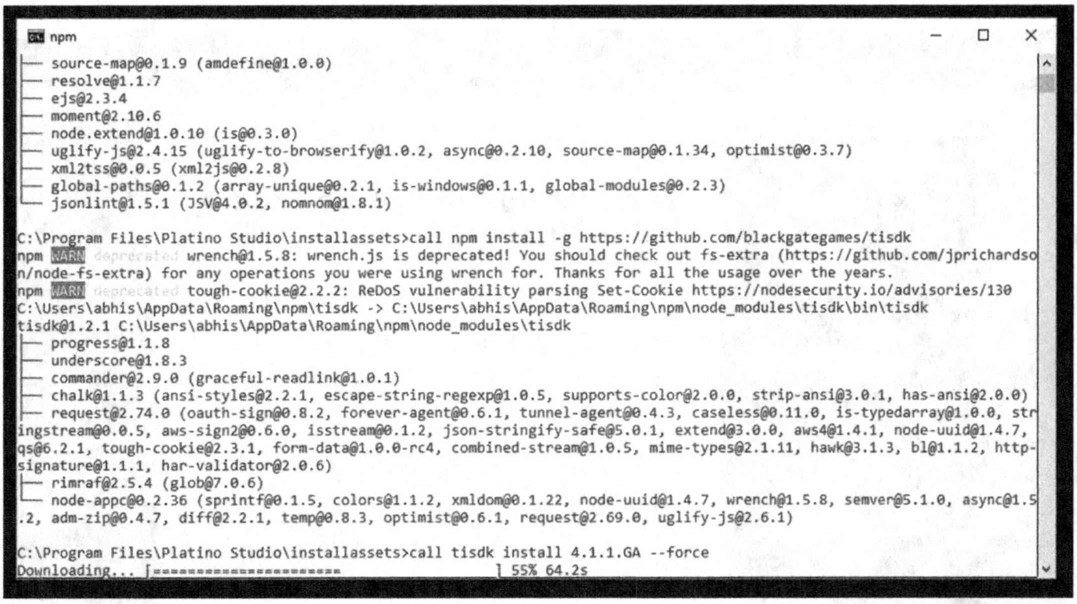

Figure 3-13. *Dependencies getting downloaded*

In the next step, you will see that all the dependencies have been installed. That download of the Titanium SDK dependencies is complete and you will get a 100% completion message in the command prompt window. This process is shown in Figure 3-14.

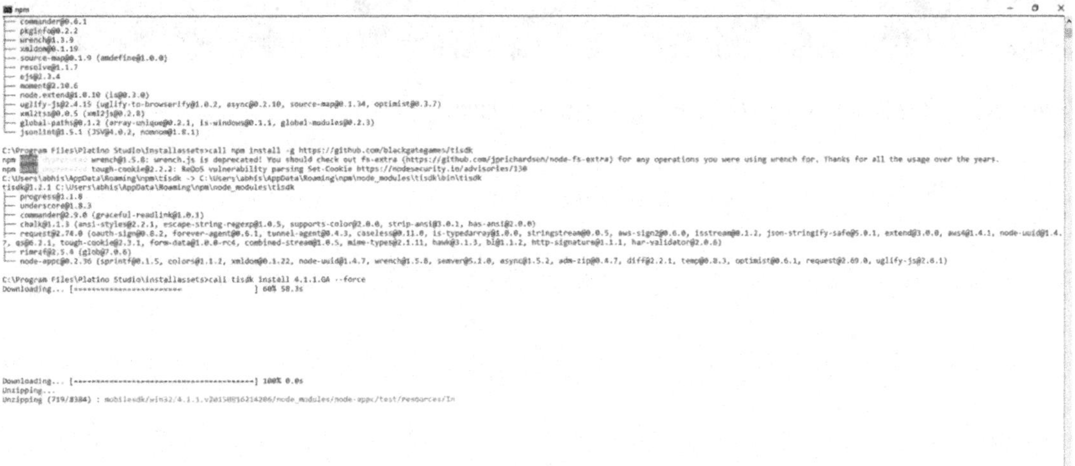

Figure 3-14. *The completed download process*

After the dependencies are installed, if installation was successful, the Platino Studio Setup Wizard will reach the final step. Simply click Finish, as shown in Figure 3-15.

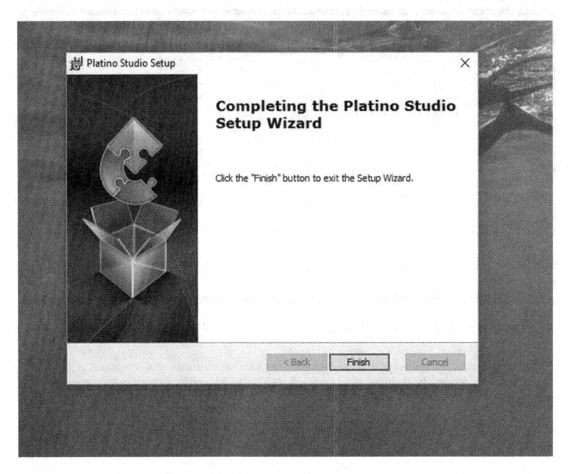

Figure 3-15. *Completing installation of the Platino game engine*

Now you can start the Platino game engine from the desktop. Once a workspace opens, click OK, as shown in Figure 3-16, to continue to use the engine.

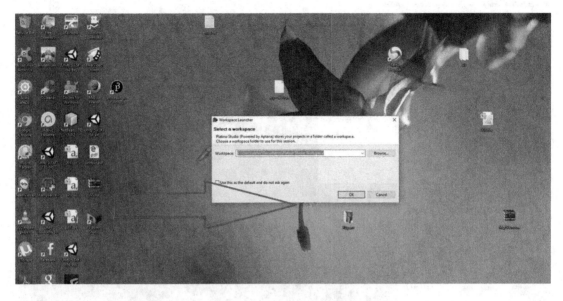

Figure 3-16. *Starting the engine*

The Platino game engine opens (Figure 3-17) and you are ready to work with your first project.

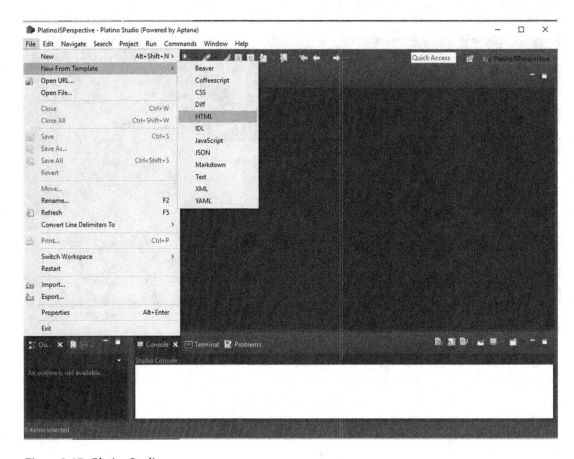

Figure 3-17. *Platino Studio*

Summary

This chapter has provided the basic steps for setting up the Platino game engine. Wizards run the configuration scripts and install the Platino game engine. In the next chapter, we will start the development process.

CHAPTER 4

Getting into Development with Platino Game Engine

In Chapter 3 we saw how to install the Platino game engine. In this chapter, we work on developing apps with it. Our primary target is to see the features of the engine and how we can take advantage of them.

Let's Make an App

We will start working on a web app first with Platino, in terms of gamification only.

When we open Game Studio, it looks like Figure 4-1.

Figure 4-1. *Platino Studio open in Windows*

In the top left corner, click File. Click New, and then click Mobile App Project, as shown in Figure 4-2.

© Abhishek Nandy and Debashree Chanda 2016
A. Nandy and D. Chanda, *Beginning Platino Game Engine*, DOI 10.1007/978-1-4842-2484-7_4

Figure 4-2. *Opening a new mobile project*

Within the mobile app project, there are several project templates. Select web and then select HTML-based Application, as shown in Figure 4-3, and then click Next.

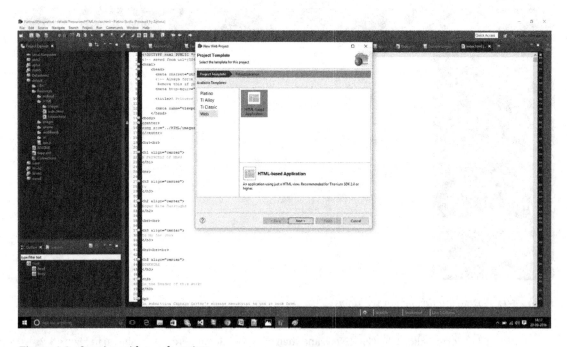

Figure 4-3. *Starting with a web project*

The next step is to name the project. In the example in Figure 4-4, the name is Debashree2. Click Finish.

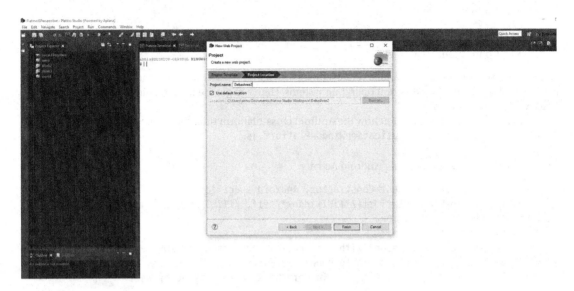

Figure 4-4. *Naming the project*

Let's take a look at Figure 4-5, which displays the file structure of the project.

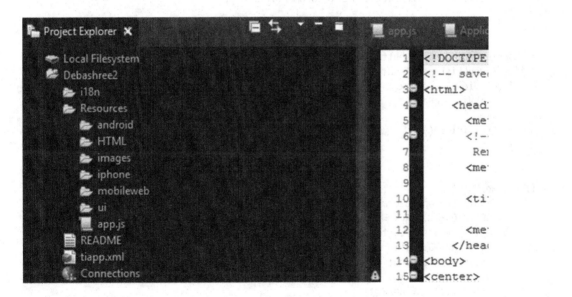

Figure 4-5. *The file structure of the project*

If you just go through the directory of the project, you can see we have these files within it.

- I18n
- Resources

- App.js
- Readme
- Tiapp.xml
- Connections

I18n is used for localization and is very useful for translation. Resources is the main location where we have definitions targeted for different operating systems. Here you get the detailed files that are required to make your app cross-platform.

Let's take a look in Listing 4-1 at how the Android cross-platform utility works and how the task is handled in the background by ApplicationWindowPlatform.js.

Listing 4-1. The Code for Handling Android Activity

```
// Application Window Component Constructor, Android specific
function ApplicationWindowPlatform(/*TiUIWindow*/self, /*TiUIView*/webView, /*boolean*/
titleBarOn, /*boolean*/drawerOn) {
    // A note about the NavBar:
    // - We use the nav bar along with some navigation buttons on iOS.
    // - We use the menu on Android to handle forward/back
    // - For mobile web, we rely on the forward/back button in the browser

    if(titleBarOn) {
        // When the webview loads, set the title and enable the left/right nav button
        webView.addEventListener('load', function(e) {
            self.title = webView.evalJS('document.title');
        });
    }

    // Handle Android back button.
    self.addEventListener('android:back', function() {
        if(webView.canGoBack()) {
            webView.goBack();
        } else {
            self.close();
        }
    });

    if (drawerOn) {
        // Create the Android menu.
        var FORWARD = 1, BACK = 2;
        var activity = self.activity;
        activity.onCreateOptionsMenu = function(e) {
            var menu = e.menu;
            var menuItem = menu.add({
                title : L('back'),
                itemId : BACK
            });
            menuItem.setIcon('/images/LeftArrow.png');
            menuItem.addEventListener('click', function(e) {
                webView.goBack();
            });
```

```
        menuItem = menu.add({
            title : L('forward'),
            itemId : FORWARD
        });
        menuItem.setIcon('/images/RightArrow.png');
        menuItem.addEventListener('click', function(e) {
            webView.goForward();
        });
    };
    activity.onPrepareOptionsMenu = function(e) {
        var menu = e.menu;
        var menuItem = menu.findItem(BACK);
        menuItem.enabled = webView.canGoBack();
        menuItem = menu.findItem(FORWARD);
        menuItem.enabled = webView.canGoForward();
    };
  }
}

module.exports = ApplicationWindowPlatform;
```

This is autogenerated code when we create the project. You see in the code that it creates the main menu and also handles the back button.

For handling phone events, you can see there are two JavaScript files generated by the project:

- `ApplicationPlatformWindow.js`

- `Drawer.js`

All are handled on the UI files of the project because the result is how the UI looks within an iOS device (see Listing 4-2).

Listing 4-2. The Code for Handling iOS Flow of an App

```
// Application Window Component Constructor, platform specific features
function ApplicationWindowPlatform(/*TiUIWindow*/self, /*TiUIView*/webView, /*boolean*/
titleBarOn, /*boolean*/drawerOn) {

    if (titleBarOn) {
        // When the webview loads, set the title
        webView.addEventListener('load', function(e) {
            self.title = webView.evalJS('document.title');
        });

    }

    if (drawerOn) {
        // Put a back/forward button into a drawer at the bottom of the screen that can be
        // opened when needed.
        var Drawer = require('/ui/Drawer');
        var drawer = new Drawer(self);
        var backButton = Ti.UI.createButton({
            backgroundImage: '/images/LeftArrow.png' ,
            width: 48,
```

```
            height: 48
    });
    backButton.addEventListener('click', function (e) {
        webView.goBack();
    });
    drawer.buttonBar.add(backButton);
    var forwardButton = Ti.UI.createButton({
        backgroundImage: '/images/RightArrow.png' ,
        width: 48,
        height: 48
    });
    forwardButton.addEventListener('click', function (e) {
        webView.goForward();
    });
    drawer.buttonBar.add(forwardButton);

    self.add(drawer.view);
    }
}

module.exports = ApplicationWindowPlatform;
```

The drawer.js file adjusts itself for different screen sizes of an iOS device, as given in Listing 4-3.

Listing 4-3. The Code for Handling iOS Device Screens

```
/ Drawer containing a button bar to drag up from the bottom of the screen by pressing the
pull tab.
var pullTabSize = { width: 48, height: 16 };
var iconSize = { width: 48, height: 48 };
var opacity = 0.75;
var speed = 500;

// Gets all the applicable sizes based on the current size of the screen, used for initial
layout and handling rotation
// @opened  boolean Indicates whether the tray should be opened or closed when determine
dimensions.
function DrawerGetLayout(/*boolean*/opened, /*boolean*/titleBarOn) {
    var screenSize = { width: Ti.Platform.displayCaps.getPlatformWidth(), height:
Ti.Platform.displayCaps.getPlatformHeight() };
    var layout = {};

    // Account for the status bar
    var offset = 20;
    // Nav bar size is the same on iPhone portrait and all iPad orientations, shorter on
    iPhone landscape
    if (titleBarOn) {
        offset += (Ti.Platform.osname == 'iphone' && screenSize.width > screenSize.height ?
        32 : 44);
    }

    layout.pullTabButton = {
```

```
            left: (screenSize.width - pullTabSize.width) / 2,
            top: 0,
            width: pullTabSize.width,
            height: pullTabSize.height
        };
        layout.buttonBar = {
            left: 0,
            top: 0,
            width: 'auto',
            height: 'auto'
        };
        layout.view = {
            left: 0,
            top: screenSize.height - pullTabSize.height - offset,
            width: screenSize.width,
            height: pullTabSize.height + iconSize.height
        };

        if (opened) {
            layout.view.top -= iconSize.height;
        }

        return layout;
    }

    function DrawerRelayout() {
        // Relayout all elements for the drawer.
        var self = this;
        var layout = DrawerGetLayout(self.opened, !self.parent.navBarHidden);

        for (var i in layout) {
            if (layout.hasOwnProperty(i)) {
                for (var j in layout[i]) {
                    if (layout[i].hasOwnProperty(j)) {
                        self[i][j] = layout[i][j];
                    }
                }
            }
        }
    }

    function Drawer(/*TiUIWindow*/parent) {
        var self = this;

        self.parent = parent;
        self.opened = false;      // Start out with the drawer closed

        // The user clicks on the pull tab to open/close the drawer.
        self.pullTabButton = Ti.UI.createButton({
            backgroundImage: '/images/PullTab.png',
            opacity: opacity
        });
```

```
        self.pullTabButton.addEventListener('click', function PullTabClick(e) {
            if (self.opened) {
                self.close();
            } else {
                self.open();
            }
        });

        // Button bar below the pull tab
        self.buttonBar = Ti.UI.createView({
            backgroundColor: 'black',
            opacity: opacity,
            layout: 'horizontal'
        });

        // High level container
        self.view = Ti.UI.createView({
            layout: 'vertical'
         });
        self.view.add(self.pullTabButton);
        self.view.add(self.buttonBar);

        // Layout all of our elements.
        self.relayout();

        // Handle orientation.
        function relayout(e) {
            self.relayout();
        }
        parent.addEventListener("close", function parentClose(e) {
            Ti.Gesture.removeEventListener("orientationchange", relayout);
        });
        Ti.Gesture.addEventListener("orientationchange", relayout);

        return self;
}

function DrawerOpen() {
    this.fireEvent('open', {source: this, type: 'open'});

    if (this.opened) {
        return;     // Already opened.
    }
    this.opened = true;

    // Slide up
    var layout = DrawerGetLayout(this.opened, !this.parent.navBarHidden);
    var animation = Ti.UI.createAnimation({
        top: layout.view.top,
        duration: speed
    });
    this.view.animate(animation);
```

```
}

function DrawerClose() {
    this.fireEvent('close', {source: this, type: 'close'});

    if (!this.opened) {
        return;      // Already closed
    }
    this.opened = false;

    // Slide down
    var layout = DrawerGetLayout(this.opened,!this.parent.navBarHidden);
    var animation = Ti.UI.createAnimation({
        top: layout.view.top,
        duration: speed
    });
    this.view.animate(animation);
}

function DrawerAddEventListener(name, func) {
    Ti.App.addEventListener('drawer.'+ name, func);
}

function DrawerRemoveEventListener(name, func) {
    Ti.App.removeEventListener('drawer.'+ name, func);
}

function DrawerFireEvent(name, obj) {
    Ti.App.fireEvent('drawer.'+ name, obj);
}

Drawer.prototype.open = DrawerOpen;
Drawer.prototype.close = DrawerClose;
Drawer.prototype.addEventListener = DrawerAddEventListener;
Drawer.prototype.removeEventListener = DrawerRemoveEventListener;
Drawer.prototype.fireEvent = DrawerFireEvent;
Drawer.prototype.relayout = DrawerRelayout;
module.exports = Drawer;
```

If we want to check for dependencies, as in Listing 4-4, we have to mention it in the app.js file. Currently it checks for the minimum Titanium version to run the application. If we have specific dependencies, we can mention them here.

Listing 4-4. The JS File for Checking Dependencies

```
/*
 * HTML Application Template:
 * A basic starting point for your application.  Mostly a blank canvas with a web view.
 *
 * In app.js, we generally take care of a few things:
 * - Bootstrap the application with any data we need
 * - Check for dependencies like device type, platform version, or network connection
```

```
* - Require and open our top-level UI component
*
*/

//bootstrap and check dependencies
if (Ti.version < 1.8 ) {
        alert('Sorry - this application template requires Titanium Mobile SDK 1.8 or
later');
} else {
        //require and open top level UI component
        var ApplicationWindow = require('ui/ApplicationWindow');
        new ApplicationWindow().open();
}
```

The `tiapp.xml` file, shown in Listing 4-5, contains all the definitions for the platform OS as well as external libraries that we are implementing. Any external library should be mentioned here; otherwise, it won't match.

Listing 4-5. The `Tiapp.xml` File

```xml
<?xml version="1.0" encoding="UTF-8"?>
<ti:app xmlns:ti="http://ti.appcelerator.org">
    <deployment-targets>
        <target device="mobileweb">true</target>
        <target device="iphone">true</target>
        <target device="ipad">true</target>
        <target device="android">true</target>
        <target device="blackberry">false</target>
    </deployment-targets>
    <sdk-version>4.1.1.GA</sdk-version>
    <id>com.appcelerator.htmltemplate</id>
    <name>HTML Template</name>
    <version>1.0</version>
    <guid>2ABF5A14-E804-4640-ADE9-773A3732ED53</guid>
    <publisher>appcelerator</publisher>
    <url>http://www.appcelerator.com</url>
    <description>not specified</description>
    <copyright>not specified</copyright>
    <icon>appicon.png</icon>
    <persistent-wifi>false</persistent-wifi>
    <prerendered-icon>false</prerendered-icon>
    <statusbar-style>default</statusbar-style>
    <statusbar-hidden>false</statusbar-hidden>
    <fullscreen>false</fullscreen>
    <navbar-hidden>false</navbar-hidden>
    <analytics>true</analytics>
    <iphone>
        <orientations device="iphone">
            <orientation>Ti.UI.PORTRAIT</orientation>
            <orientation>Ti.UI.UPSIDE_PORTRAIT</orientation>
            <orientation>Ti.UI.LANDSCAPE_LEFT</orientation>
            <orientation>Ti.UI.LANDSCAPE_RIGHT</orientation>
```

```
        </orientations>
        <orientations device="ipad">
            <orientation>Ti.UI.PORTRAIT</orientation>
            <orientation>Ti.UI.UPSIDE_PORTRAIT</orientation>
            <orientation>Ti.UI.LANDSCAPE_LEFT</orientation>
            <orientation>Ti.UI.LANDSCAPE_RIGHT</orientation>
        </orientations>
    </iphone>
    <android xmlns:android="http://schemas.android.com/apk/res/android"/>
    <modules/>
</ti:app>
```

Let's run the default app on a web browser first. Figure 4-6 shows the app rendered in Mozilla Firefox.

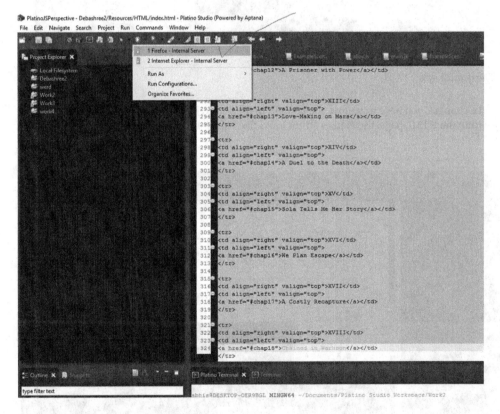

Figure 4-6. *The app rendered in Firefox*

The output of the default app looks like Figure 4-7.

Figure 4-7. *The default app*

As you make changes, you have to remove the content in the index.html page. When you have added the script tag within the HTML page, the Platino editor looks like Figure 4-8.

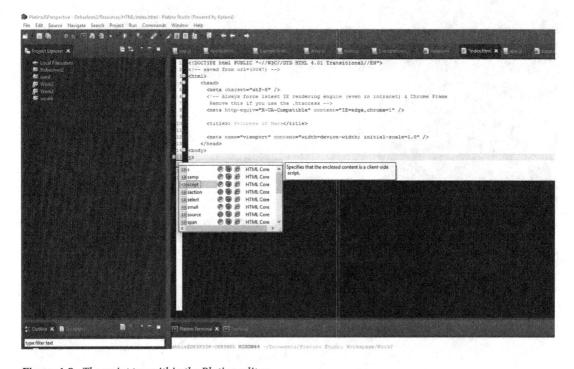

Figure 4-8. *The script tag within the Platino editor*

Now you will create a *Matrix*-like screensaver effect in our default app by making changes inside the index.html page. I was just hovering around and with a little bit of tinkering made some changes to the initial code of the open source JavaScript available.

First, take a look at the code in Listing 4-6 and then implement it inside the Platino engine.

Listing 4-6. The 20 Lines of JavaScript for a Matrix-Like Effect

```
<script>
var d=document,a=255/2,el=d.createElement('canvas');
el.width=800;el.height=600;d.body.appendChild(el);
var columns=Array(300).join().split(','),draw=requestAnimationFrame;
var ctx=el.getContext('2d'),random=Math.random,
s=Math.sin,p=parseInt;ctx.translate(el.width, 0);ctx.scale(-1,1);
function getColour(f){
return 'rgb('+[p(s(3*f)*a+a),p(s(3*f+2)*a+a),p(s(3*f+4)*a+a)].join(',')+')';}
// Apparently this algorithm is quite popular out there on the Internet
function fill(now) {
  ctx.fillStyle='rgba(0,0,0,.05)';
  ctx.fillRect(0,0,el.width,el.height);
  ctx.fillStyle=getColour(now);
  columns.map(function(y, index){
    text = String.fromCharCode(12448+random()*96);
    ctx.fillText(text, (index * 10)+10, (y||0));
    columns[index]=(y||0) > 100 + random()*1e4? 0 : y+10;
  });
  draw(fill);
}
draw(fill);

</script>
```

After adding the code and then running the app in Firefox, it looks like Figure 4-9.

Figure 4-9. The app producing the effect

The code works like this: The create element creates a canvas element and declares the width and height of the canvas. It then appends a child node. The function getColour helps in generating random color to the format and fill (now) generates the effect.

Building a Core Platino App

In this section you will build an app using the core Platino template. Open the Platino game engine, then select a mobile project. Select the Platino template and then click Platino Classic (see Figure 4-10). Name the project, and then you are ready to start. Then click Next.

Figure 4-10. *The Platino Classic template*

The project in the example shown in Figure 4-11 is named abhi2. Click Finish.

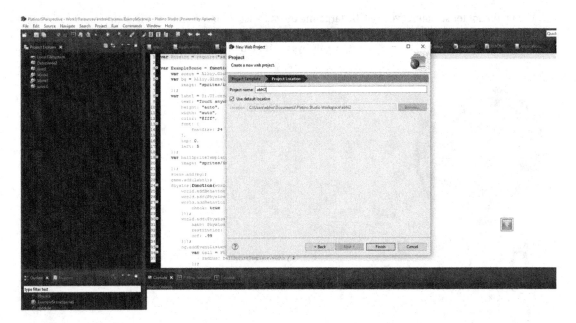

Figure 4-11. *Give the project a name*

Platino will go through the steps to create the file structure, as shown in Figure 4-12.

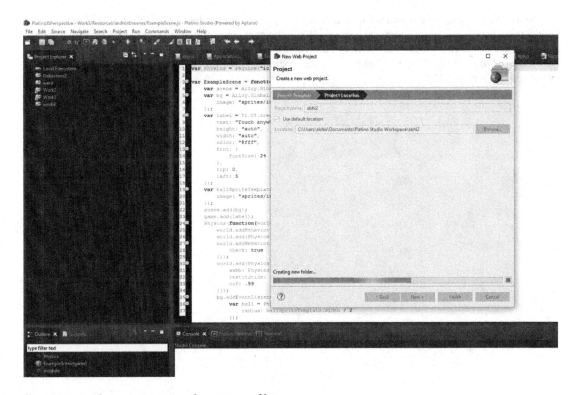

Figure 4-12. *The project creating the necessary files*

Within the folder structure, you will be targeting the start scene or the main scene of the app.

For this app, you download an Intel Software Innovator logo (Figure 4-13), which you will be using in the app. Being an Intel Software Innovators, we always wanted to include the logo.

Figure 4-13. *The Intel Software Innovator logo*

To use Platino, you need to call the module (`'io.platino'`). Remember that with the new Platino Studio, there have been many beneficial changes. When the game view function is launched, its first creates a scene in the game. You declare the scene and then create the entire structure for the app.

You need to create a folder (see Figure 4-14) where you will store the image you downloaded. Name the folder Images (Figure 4-15).

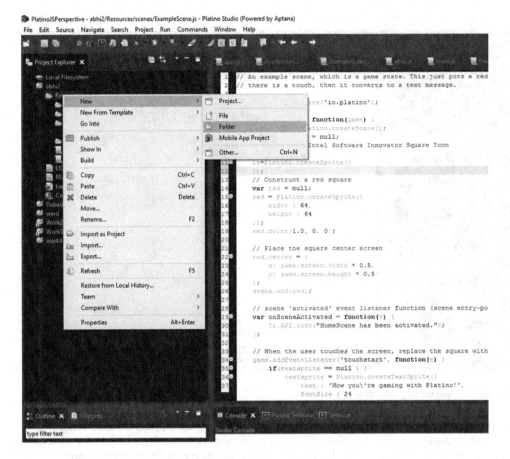

Figure 4-14. *Creating a folder for storing images*

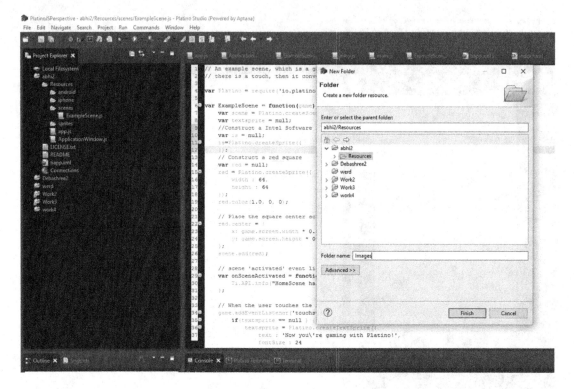

Figure 4-15. *Naming the folder you created*

Let's get the extra details of the app that we want to implement. You scale the Intel Software Innovator image to the center of the screen. Declare the sprite as is and use the create sprite method. Next, declare the path of the image and the size and width of it. Declare both as 100, then center the Intel Software Innovator icon and add the scene for rendering. The next logic is triggered when the user touches the screen: The logo disappears and a text message is shown. For this text message we have used text sprite. Let's take a look at the code, shown in Listing 4-7.

Listing 4-7. The Code for the App

```
// An example scene, which is a game state. This just puts the Intel Software Innovator
graphic on the screen until
// there is a touch, then it converts to a text message.

var Platino = require('io.platino');

var ExampleScene = function(game) {
        var scene = Platino.createScene();
        var textsprite = null;
        //Construct a Intel Software Innovator Square Icon
        var is = null;
        is=Platino.createSprite({
```

```
            image:"Images/is.jpg",
            width : 100,
                    height : 100


            });

            //Place Intel Software Innovator logo to center of the scene
            is.center = {
                    x: game.screen.width * 0.5,
                    y: game.screen.height * 0.5
            };Core Platino APPcode for app
            scene.add(is);

            // scene 'activated' event listener function (scene entry-point)
            var onSceneActivated = function(e) {
                    Ti.API.info("HomeScene has been activated.");
            };

            // When the user touches the screen, replace the logo  with a message
            game.addEventListener('touchstart', function(e) {
                    if(textsprite == null ) {
                            textsprite = Platino.createTextSprite({
                                    text : 'Now you\'re gaming with Platino!',
                                    fontSize : 24
                            });
                            textsprite.color(1.0, 1.0, 1.0);
                            textsprite.center = {
                                    x: game.screen.width * 0.5,
                                    y: game.screen.height * 0.5
                            };
                            scene.remove(is);
                            scene.add(textsprite);
                    }
            });

            // scene 'deactivated' event listener function (scene exit-point)
            var onSceneDeactivated = function(e) {
                    Ti.API.info("HomeScene has been deactivated.");
            };

            // Scene activation events here
            scene.addEventListener('activated', onSceneActivated);
            scene.addEventListener('deactivated', onSceneDeactivated);

            return scene;
}

module.exports = ExampleScene;
```

For the next app we build, you will be using the Alloy and Platino with Physics JS. To start with, let us see what Physics JS does.

Physics JS

Physics JS (Figure 4-16) is a very easy-to-use, flexible physics engine for JavaScript with many capabilities.

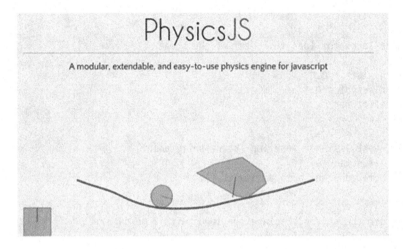

Figure 4-16. Physics JS

Let's start the project template now. Choose the Platino with Alloy template as shown in Figure 4-17. Click Next and name the project abhi4.

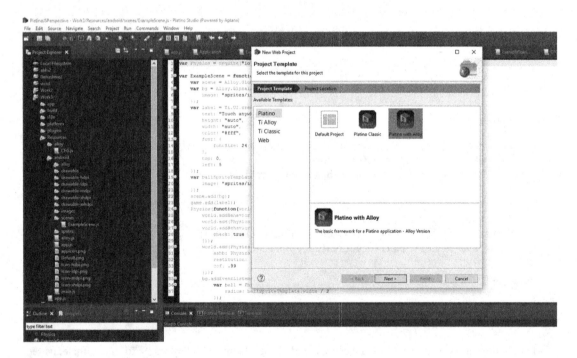

Figure 4-17. Including the Platino with Alloy template

Figure 4-18 provides a look at the folder structure.

Figure 4-18. *Project folder structure*

Okay

The app that we created has a different folder structure than the previous apps we created to this point. The folder structure and the details are given below.

- Assets

- Controllers

- Models

- Styles

- Views

- Alloy.js

- Plugins

- The other file structures are the same.

Assets

The Assets folder contains all the important files for structuring the app. It also contains details for targeting different versions. The important subfolder within the Assets folder is the Scene folder, where you write the logic for how the scene looks and, if required, to perform transitions from one scene to other. Within the sprites we keep the sprite sheets in place. The main JavaScript file contains the scene setup and the general game flow. The file looks like Listing 4-8.

Listing 4-8. The main.js File

```
// Start place of your application. Generally used for control of the scene setup and
general game flow.

// Create and set up the game
var game = Alloy.Globals.Platino.createGameView();
game.fps = 30;
game.color(0, 0, 0);
game.debug = false; // disables debug logs (not to be used for production)
game.enableOnDrawFrameEvent = false; // optimization: setting to 'false' disables
'enterframe' event
game.screen = {width: 480, height: 320};

// Load the scene and start the game
game.addEventListener('onload', function(e) {
        var scene = require("scenes/ExampleScene");
        game.pushScene(new scene(game));
        game.start();
});
Module.exports = game;
```

The Controllers folder contains two files: index.js and window.js. The index.js file, shown in Listing 4-9, redirects to the window controller for better naming conventions.

Listing 4-9. The index.js File

```
// Redirect to the window controller for better naming conventions
var window = Alloy.createController('window').getView();
window.open();
```

The window.js file contains the logic that imports the main file (see Listing 4-10), which must return a game object.

Listing 4-10. The main.js File

```
// Import the main file, which must return a game object. This is simply added to our window
and we start.
// The window can be set up in window.tss

var game = require('main');
$.win.add(game);
$.win.open();

// Free up game resources when window is closed
$.win.addEventListener('close', function(e) {
        game = null;
});
```

The next important file in the structure is the alloy.js file, shown in Listing 4-11, which binds the Platino API.

Listing 4-11. The Content of the `alloy.js` File

```
// The Platino API can be accessed via Alloy.Globals.Platino from any controller file. This
makes it an automatic
// include. If you want to create other globals, the Alloy.Globals namespace is meant for
just that.

Alloy.Globals.Platino = require('io.platino');
```

The demo that we are working on right now will first show the Intel Software Innovator logo. When we touch the screen, the logo overlaps with the background of Platino and gives the count. We will be using the Platino background logo shown in Figure 4-19 for the app.

Figure 4-19. *The Platino background screen*

First you need to add Physics JS inside the `Tiapp.xml` so you can use Physics JS within Platino (see Listing 4-12).

Listing 4-12. The Code for the Game

```
var Physics = require('io.platino.physicsjs');

var ExampleScene = function(game) {
        // Scene setup
        var scene = Alloy.Globals.Platino.createScene();
        var bg = Alloy.Globals.Platino.createSprite({image: 'sprites/bg.png'});
        var label = Ti.UI.createLabel({text: "Touch anywhere", height: 'auto', width:
        'auto', color:'#fff', font:{fontSize:24}, top: 0, left: 5});
        var ballSpriteTemplate = Alloy.Globals.Platino.createSprite({image: 'sprites/1.
        png'}); // For knowing its size
        scene.add(bg);
        game.add(label);

        // Physics
          Physics(function(world){
                // Gravity
                world.addBehavior( Physics.behavior('constant-acceleration'));

                // Bouncing
                world.add( Physics.behavior('body-impulse-response') );

                // Rigid bodies
                world.addBehavior( Physics.behavior('body-collision-detection',
                {check:true}));

                // World boundaries
                world.add(Physics.behavior('edge-collision-detection', {
                    aabb: Physics.aabb(0, 0, game.screen.width, game.screen.height),
                    restitution: 0.99,
                    cof: 0.99
                }));

                // The user can click anywhere on the background to drop a ball
                bg.addEventListener('touchstart', function(e) {
                        // Create the ball as only a physics object
                        var ball = Physics.body('circle', { radius: ballSpriteTemplate.width
                        / 2 });

                        // Position the physics object
                        ball.state.pos.x = e.x;
                        ball.state.pos.y = e.y;

                        // Make sure the world acts upon the ball
                        world.add(ball);

                        // Set the label to balls total
                        label.text = "Total Intel Software Innovator logos: " + world.
                        getBodies().length;
```

```
                    // Associate a platino sprite with the physics body
                    ball.sprite = Alloy.Globals.Platino.createSprite({image: 'sprites/1.
                    png', centerX: e.x, centerY: e.y});
                    scene.add(ball.sprite);
            });

            // Once per frame, step the world and apply each physics object's position
            to its referenced sprite
            game.addEventListener('enterframe', function(e) {
                    world.stepDelta(e.delta);
            });
    });

    return scene;
};

module.exports = ExampleScene;
```

Now let us compile the project for an Android build. Attach your Android phone with debugging mode on, and then open Platino Studio. Click Run As, then select Android Device, as shown in Figure 4-20.

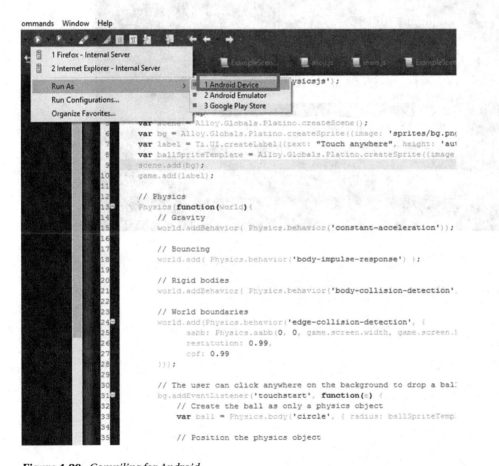

Figure 4-20. *Compiling for Android*

The compilation process will go through steps, as shown in Figure 4-21.

Figure 4-21. *Series of steps for compiling the project*

When the compilation is complete, you will see the app runs on the device. If there is an exception, you will get an error message both on the phone as well as the integrated development environment (IDE). The error might occur because we haven't added the Physics JS module as shown in Figure 4-22 in runtime.

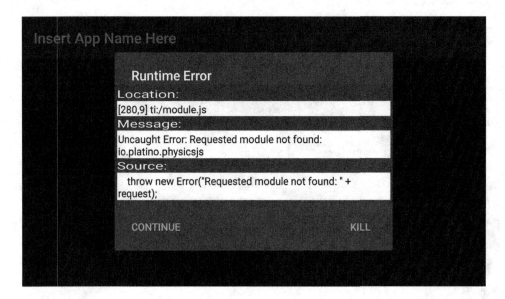

Figure 4-22. *Runtime error*

The app when installed on a phone looks like Figure 4-23.

Figure 4-23. *The app as it is shown on a mobile device*

When it is running properly, the app looks something like Figure 4-24.

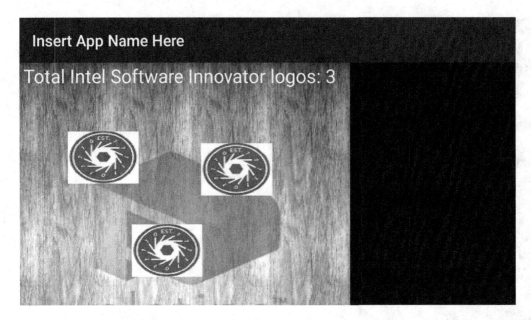

Figure 4-24. *The app running on a mobile device*

In this chapter, you have seen some simple use cases of the Platino engine. You can take it further by adding more functionalities to the app.

Summary

In this chapter we have shown how to develop apps with Platino Studio. We have shown the templates and how you can take advantage of them. We have also shown how to implement Physics JS within the module.

■ ■ ■

CHAPTER 5

Creative Coding and Processing

In Chapter 4, we went through the process for developing games with the Platino game engine. You have seen how we use the game engine features to work in different interactive ways in a game engine. We move ahead in this chapter and introduce creative coding.

Creative Coding and Processing

In this chapter, we start with creative coding. We first define the term and then move ahead with different frameworks for creative coding. We next focus on the creative coding language we are going to cover, Processing. We provide an introduction to Processing and show how the language has evolved, detail support for different platforms, and cover installing Processing in Windows.

The following topics are covered in this chapter:

- Creative coding and different frameworks.

- Processing language.

- Different platform support and installation on Windows.

- We demonstrate with examples and build it for Android.

What Is Creative Coding?

Creative coding, as the name suggests, is an unusual way of representing our code. It is the combination of arts with code. Creative coding helps us in several ways. The styles are as follows:

- Art installations in Billboards.

- Projection mapping.

- Special installation through interactive gestures.

Art Installations

Art installations are representations using 3D visualizing techniques and creative coding as the programming base (see Figure 5-1). The programming language generally used in art installations is Processing (which we introduce later). Art installation changes the perception of free space with projects brought about by creative coding. Art installations can be temporary or permanent. Some art installations that are permanent can be 3D printed after we have coded them with creative coding techniques.

© Abhishek Nandy and Debashree Chanda 2016

A. Nandy and D. Chanda, *Beginning Platino Game Engine*, DOI 10.1007/978-1-4842-2484-7_5

Figure 5-1. *Art installations*

Projection Mapping

Projection mapping is a technique with which we turn an everyday object, say a wall or a building, into a surface that displays different visualizations with an awesome effect.

The general structure of projection mapping is shown in Figure 5-2.

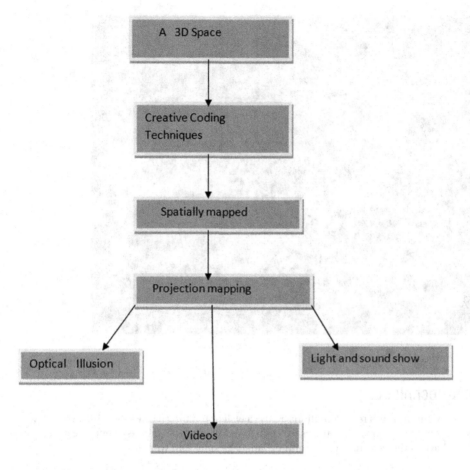

Figure 5-2. *Projection mapping flow*

A 3D Space

A 3D space can be a wall or a building where we set up our projection tools and then analyze the space on which we will perform the projection. This 3D space acts as carrier for producing the effect. Figure 5-3 shows how a corridor of 3D space has been transformed by a sparkling art installation effect.

Figure 5-3. *Creative coding installations*

Creative Coding Techniques

Now, before we project visual arts and representations across a wall or building (see Figures 5-4 and 5-5), we first must to find out which programming languages we need to work with to get our task done. We cover the options, and then you have to choose which programming language suits your work best.

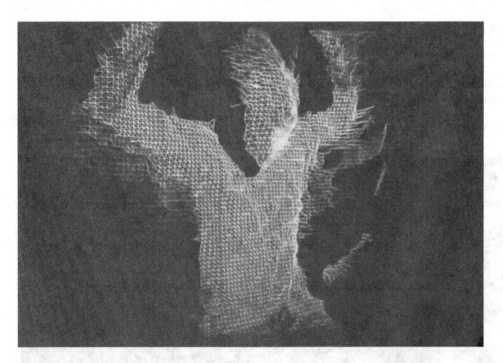

Figure 5-4. *Unique styling effect*

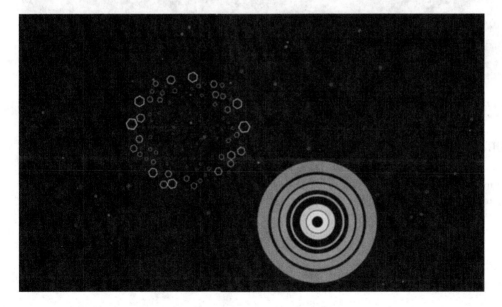

Figure 5-5. *Creative coding patterns*

Spatial Mapping

As you can see, according to the space, you can create projections suitable for a particular geometric body or bodies within the frame to be applied. This projection is made easy using algorithms that identify the geometric body, and mapping helps the creative programming language to produce the desired effect. Projection generally happens with powerful 3D projectors and uses cameras that support 3D scanning, which helps in getting things in order.

Figure 5-6 shows spatial mapping in Hololens.

Figure 5-6. *Spatial mapping using Hololens*

Projection Mapping

Now with everything in place, you have to perform the projection with all the things just discussed to produce a stunning effect. The virtual art piece is very engaging, and can also be triggered by voice or gestures. Figure 5-7 shows an amazing art effect at the Sydney Opera House.

Figure 5-7. *Amazing art installations at the Sydney Opera House*

Examples of Projection Mapping

As we create different projection mapping patterns, there are different variants of them, such as optical illusion, videos, and light and sound shows.

Sketching to Reality

In science fiction movies, we see a lot of objects and scenarios that are very eye-catching and very extraordinary. Creative coding helps us bring those ideas to life. For example, Conway's game of life, displayed in Figure 5-8, can be brought into life with the help of creative coding.

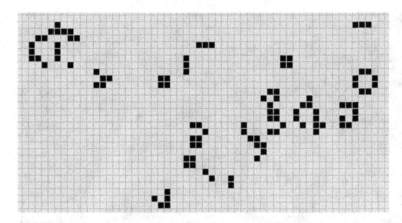

Figure 5-8. *Conway's game of life*

This is an algorithm proposed by John Horton Conway based on cellular automata to give an overview of how the biological functionalities of life occur. This is a perfect simulation that happens in a 2D grid and provides a very close to life-like effect.

As things get more intriguing, we now introduce you to different frameworks.

Different Frameworks

In this section we introduce you to different creative coding frameworks that are very useful in creative coding.

Cinder

Cinder (Figure 5-9) is a creative coding framework specially meant for C++. The best way to keep updated with Cinder is through a combination of Cinder and GIT. In this case, you will always get updates very easily. The platform support for Cinder is Windows and OSX.

Figure 5-9. *Cinder logo*

You can download Cinder from https://libcinder.org/download, as depicted in Figure 5-10.

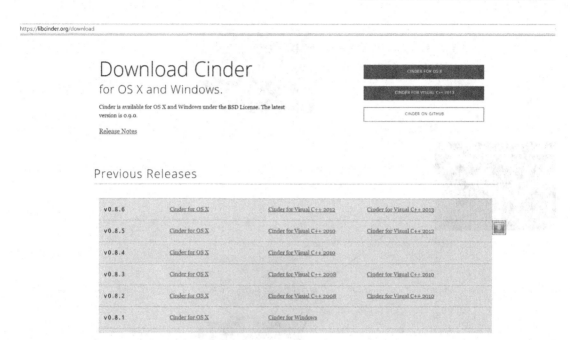

Figure 5-10. *Downloading Cinder*

When you download Cinder, it generally comes in the form of a zip file, which is displayed in Figure 5-11.

Figure 5-11. *The zip file for Cinder*

Some helpful tools are available for Cinder that allow us to add additional libraries into the package. These different tools are shown in Figure 5-12.

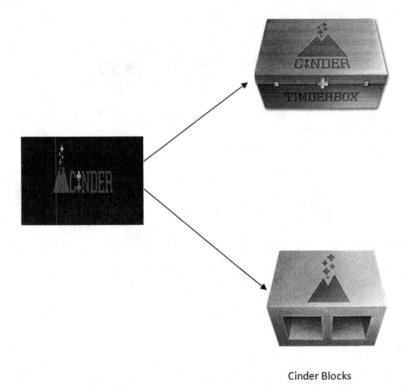

Cinder Blocks

Figure 5-12. *Cinder tools for adding libraries*

Tinderbox

Tinderbox is a tool that is designed to create a simplified structure for creating new projects. It can create both Visual Studio and Xcode projects and also integrate CinderBlocks.

CinderBlocks

CinderBlocks is a prepackaged collection of libraries and code that allows for third-party libraries.

Let's cover how to get started with CinderBlocks. Navigate to the Cinder folder and find the Tools folder, as shown in Figure 5-13.

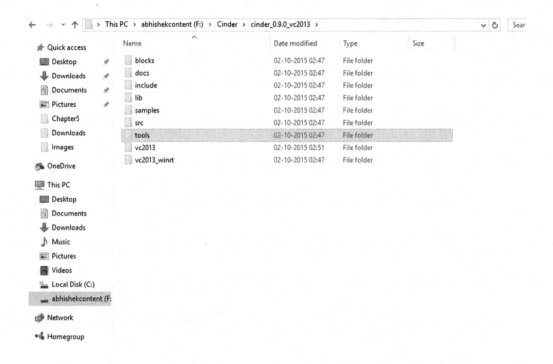

Figure 5-13. *The Tools subfolder within the Cinder main folder*

Open the Tools folder to find the TinderBox-Win folder, seen in Figure 5-14.

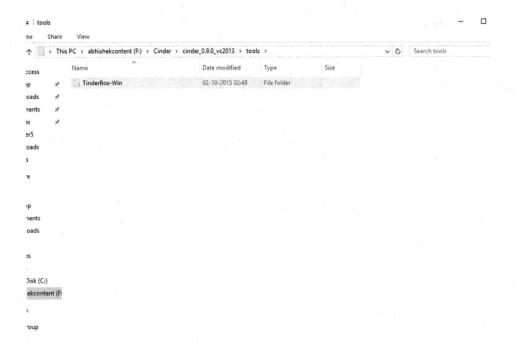

Figure 5-14. *The TinderBox-Win folder*

Now launch the `TinderBox.exe` file to run the application, as shown in Figure 5-15.

Figure 5-15. *Opening the `TinderBox.exe` file*

Select the Basic template option with Visual Studio 2013 and click Next, as seen in Figure 5-16.

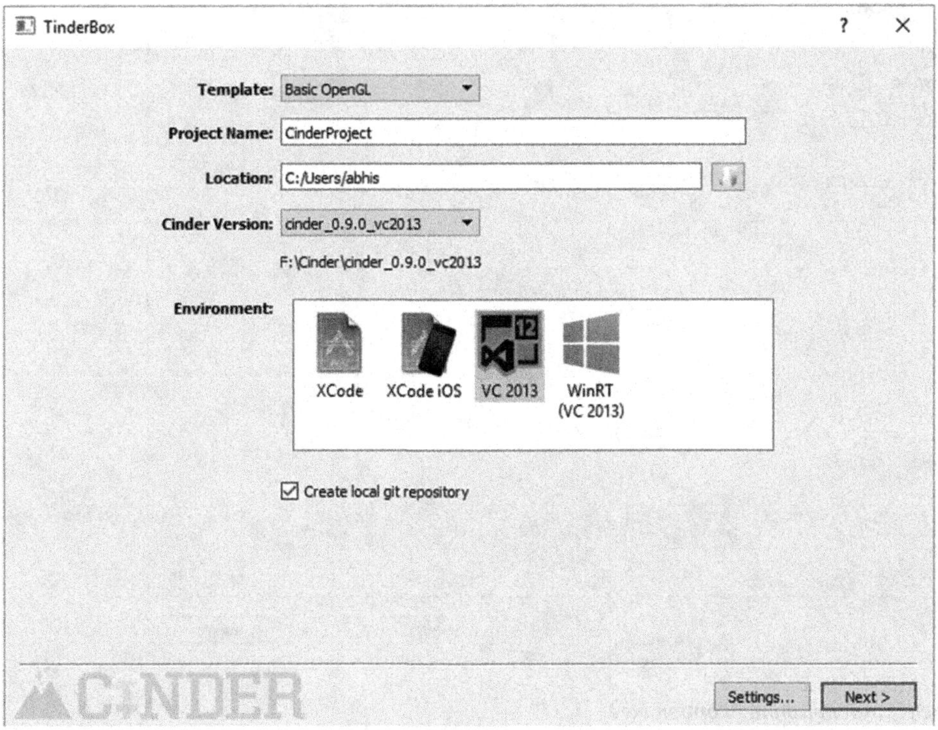

Figure 5-16. *The project options with TinderBox*

Now you can set up environment options for the project, as depicted in Figure 5-17.

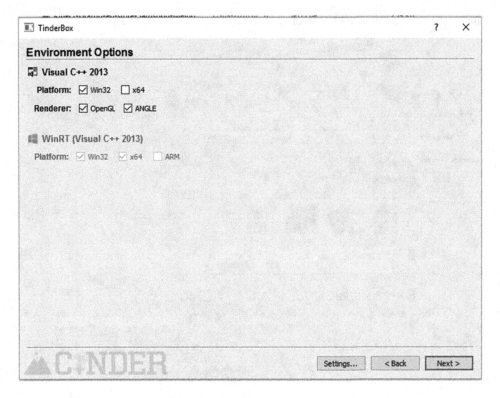

Figure 5-17. *Select the environment option here*

In the next step, shown in Figure 5-18, you can add third-party libraries.

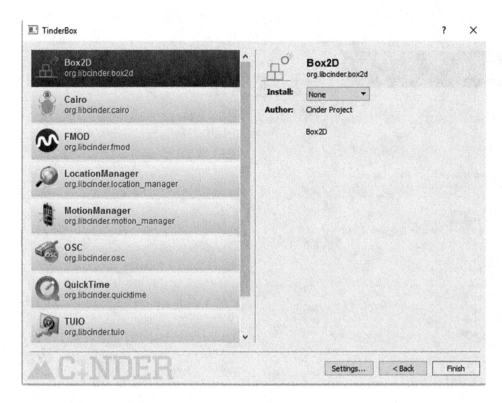

Figure 5-18. *Select a third-party library*

From the list of avalable libraries, select the one you want to install and then click Finish, as shown in Figure 5-19.

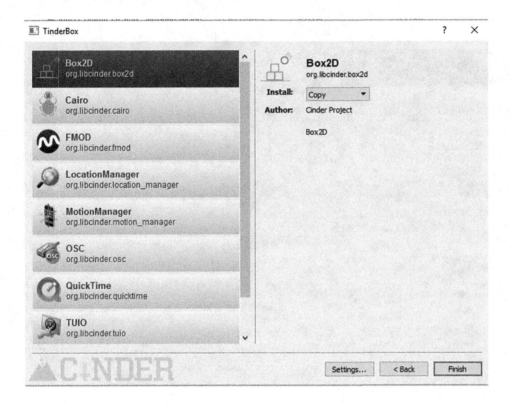

Figure 5-19. *Selecting the Box2D library*

This results in a folder structure that you can open in Microsoft Visual Studio 2013, which is displayed in Figure 5-20.

Name	Date modified	Type	Size
.git	17-09-2016 15:06	File folder	
assets	17-09-2016 15:06	File folder	
blocks	17-09-2016 15:06	File folder	
include	17-09-2016 15:06	File folder	
resources	17-09-2016 15:06	File folder	
src	17-09-2016 15:06	File folder	
vc2013	17-09-2016 15:06	File folder	

Figure 5-20. *The file structure for Visual Studio 2013*

What Can We Do with Cinder?

Cinder helps in several domains and brings the aspect of creative coding to its full potential. Figure 5-21 shows the wide variety of uses for which we can implement it.

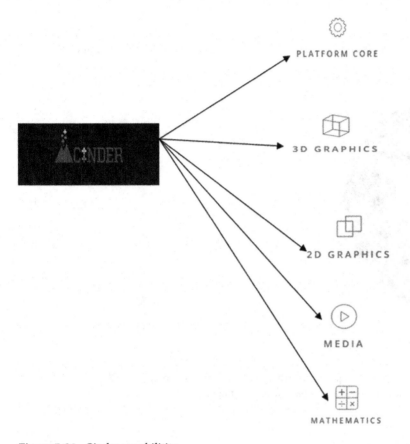

Figure 5-21. *Cinder capabilities*

Let's have a brief look at the details.

- *Platform core*: Stand-alone Mac and PC applications (platform-native Windows and event handling done), C++ Core, screensavers, Internet I/O, multitouch, UI events, and communication APIs.

- *3D graphics*: Core classes (perspective and orthographic cameras, triangle meshes, OBJ loading, and geometric primitives).

- OpenGL core, OpenGL classes, geometry synthesis, and GUI parameters.

- *2D graphics*: Robust image I/O, image processing, HDR imaging, powerful 2D rasterizer, fonts, and text.

- *Media*: Video capture, open CV, full-featured QuickTime, audio I/O, modular audio nodes, and audio processing.

- *Mathematics*: GLM math primitives, utilities, and geometric primitives.

Now that we've provided an introduction to Cinder, let's move to the details about another C++ framework, openFrameworks.

openFrameworks

One of the most important frameworks and a good utility toolkit for creative coding is openFrameworks (Figure 5-22).

Figure 5-22. *openFrameworks*

The openFrameworks home page (`http://openframeworks.cc/`) is shown in Figure 5-23. All of the details about downloading the framework are available from this page.

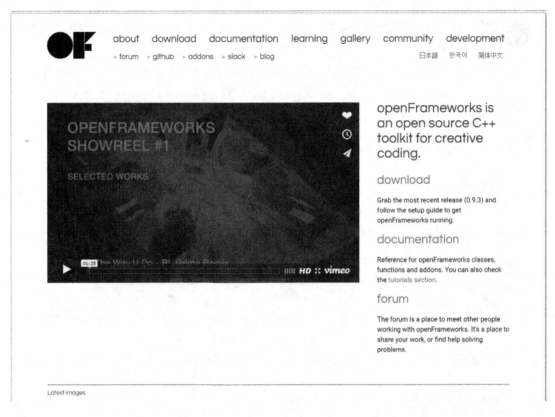

Figure 5-23. *The openFrameworks home page*

An excellent feature of openFrameworks is that it is available in Windows, OSX, Linux, Android, and JavaScript (through ECMA 6.0). The download options on the main page are shown in Figure 5-24.

Figure 5-24. *openFrameworks download options*

We will set openFrameworks to operate on a Windows platform using Microsoft Visual Studio 2015. The download package is also available using the Visual Studio Gallery, shown in Figure 5-25. It is the openFrameworks plug-in that we have to download.

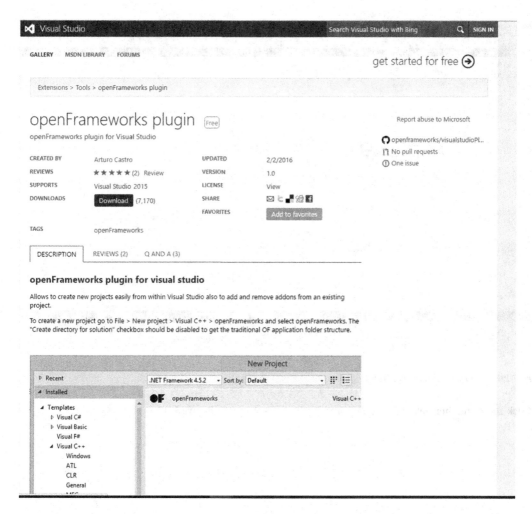

Figure 5-25. *Downloading the openFrameworks plug-in*

You can now go through the steps to set up openFrameworks in Visual Studio 2015. First, launch Visual Studio 2015, as shown in Figure 5-26.

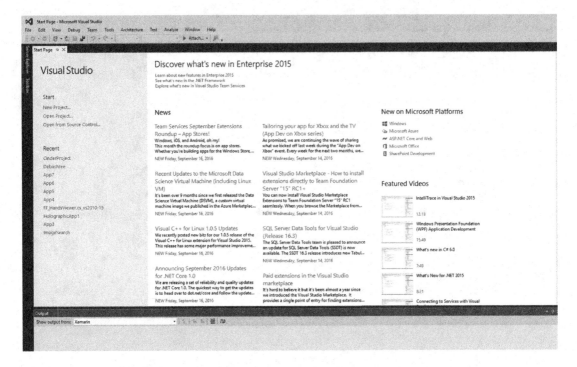

Figure 5-26. *Visual Studio Start page*

Click Tools and then select Extensions and Updates, as shown in Figure 5-27.

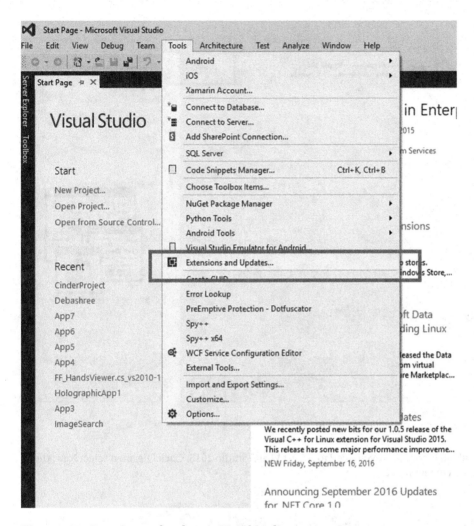

Figure 5-27. Extensions and updates in Visual Studio

Next you need to find openFrameworks within the Extensions and Updates list. Click Download to download the plug-in, as depicted in Figure 5-28.

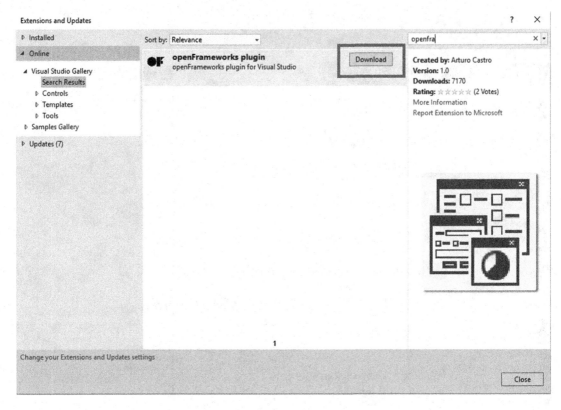

Figure 5-28. openFrameworks download plug-in option

After the download is complete, you need to restart Visual Studio 2015. Click File, then select New, then Project, as highlighted in Figure 5-29.

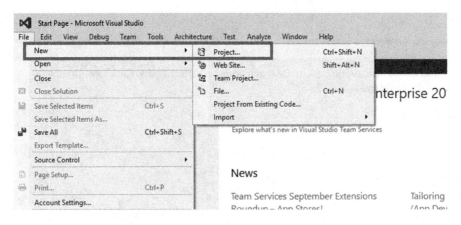

Figure 5-29. Opening a new project in Visual Studio 2015

Select the openFrameworks template option from the C++ templates. This template allows us to create a creative coding project within Visual Studio 2015. Name the project OpenFrame1, as shown in Figure 5-30.

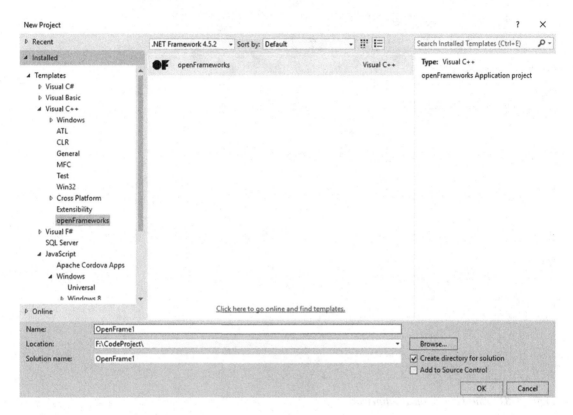

Figure 5-30. *Naming the project OpenFrame1*

Click OK to open the project. It will next look for openFrameworks that we have to install from the Web (see Figure 5-31).

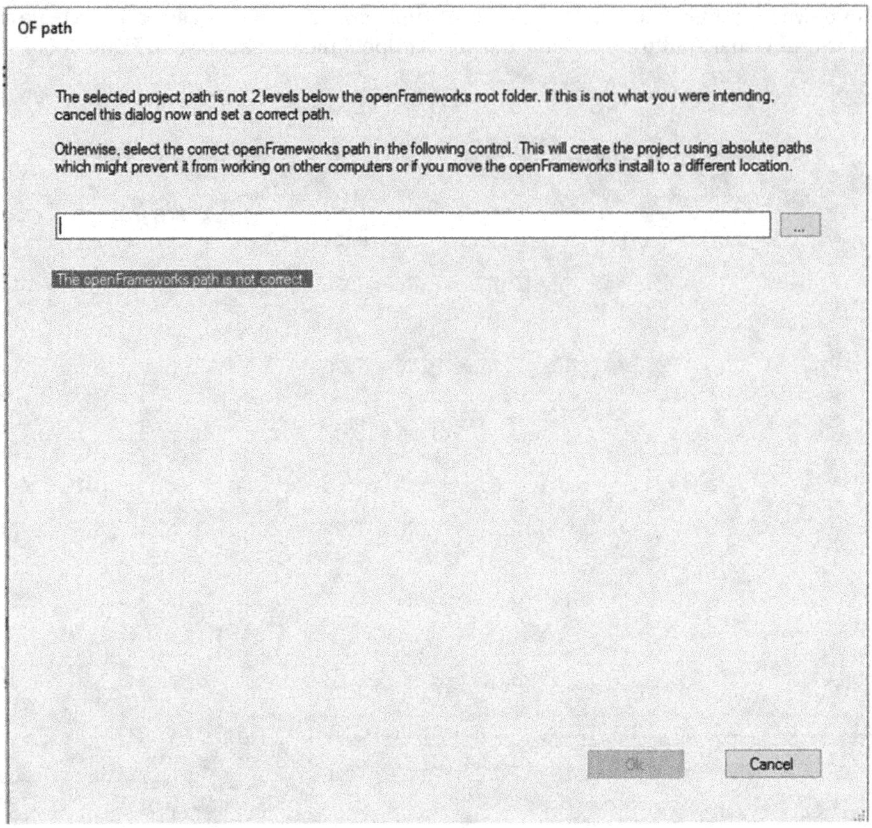

Figure 5-31. *Checking for openFrameworks path*

After you extract the downloaded framework, you must select the correct path, as in Figure 5-32.

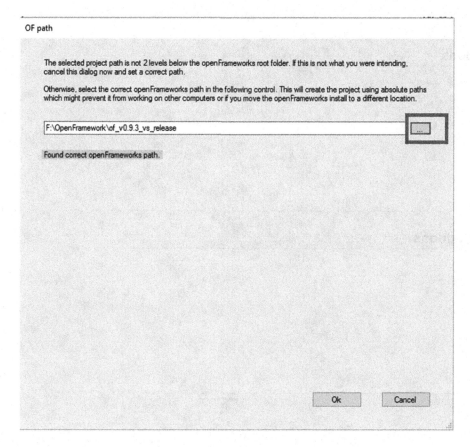

Figure 5-32. *Select the right path for openFrameworks*

When you click OK, you are presented with numerous add-on options, as depicted in Figure 5-33.

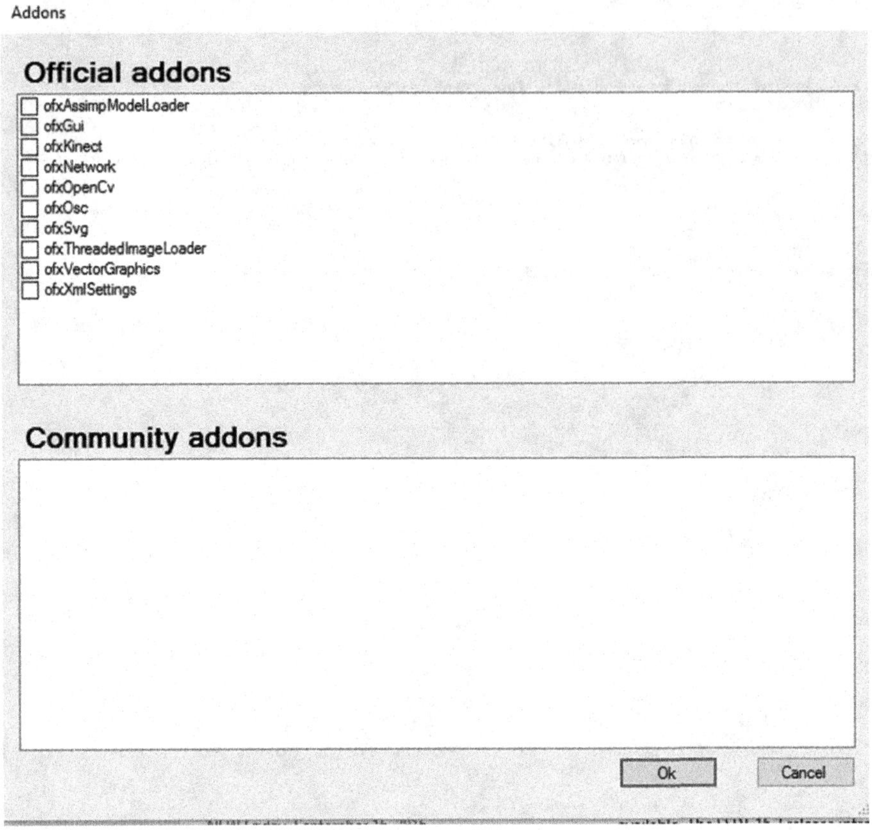

Addons

Official addons

- [ ] ofxAssimpModelLoader
- [ ] ofxGui
- [ ] ofxKinect
- [ ] ofxNetwork
- [ ] ofxOpenCv
- [ ] ofxOsc
- [ ] ofxSvg
- [ ] ofxThreadedImageLoader
- [ ] ofxVectorGraphics
- [ ] ofxXmlSettings

Community addons

```
            Ok        Cancel
```

Figure 5-33. *Selecting add-ons*

Select the desired add-ons and then click OK to create a simple project, as shown in Figure 5-34.

Figure 5-34. *Selecting the appropriate add-ons*

In the Solution Explorer for Visual Studio, shown in Figure 5-35, the entire openFrameworks option is available.

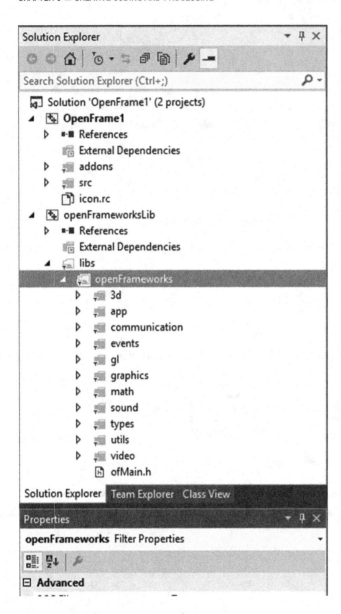

Figure 5-35. *The openFrameworks option*

You can then run the app, as shown in Figure 5-36.

Figure 5-36. *Running the app*

If the dialog box indicates that a project is out of date, click Yes to build it, as shown in Figure 5-37.

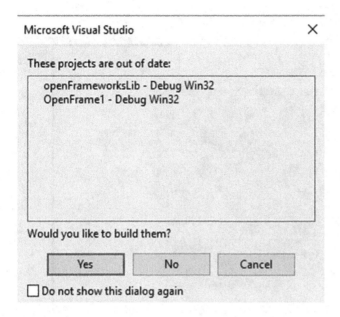

Figure 5-37. *Building projects that are out of date*

In the next, section we start discussing Processing as a creative coding language and also extend it further. Add a window resizing option to the setup function (see Listing 5-1) so that when we run the app, the app window resizes.

Listing 5-1. Adding Window Resizing Logic

```
void ofApp::setup(){
        ofSetWindowShape(500, 500);
        ofSetWindowPosition(10, 10);

}
```

We also add a logic for a key pressed event, as shown in Listing 5-2.

Listing 5-2. Key Pressed Event

```
void ofApp::keyPressed(int key){
        char str[] = "Hello OpenFramework";

        cout << "Value of str is : " << str << endl;

}
```

The output for the project is displayed in Figure 5-38.

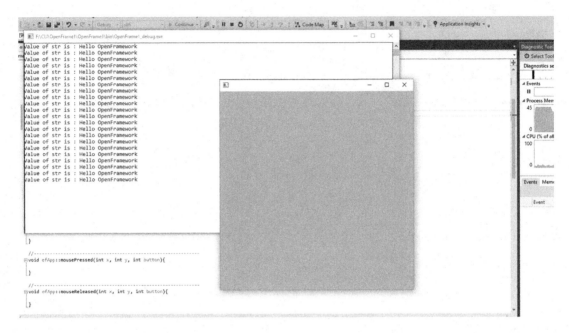

Figure 5-38. *The output for the project*

Processing

Processing (see Figure 5-39) is a programming language specially intended for creative coding. The most important part of Processing as a language is that it brings visual arts to life with the help of coding. It helps us to learn the fundamentals of computer programming by actually showing it visually.

Figure 5-39. *Processing icon*

Processing is an open source language that can run on multiple platforms. We can easily get going inside a processing environment in Windows, Linux, or Mac. It is an IDE in which we program and the output is a visual interpretation of the code we write. Everything we code in Processing is considered a sketch. The extension of a file that is saved in Processing is *.pde. Another important aspect of Processing is its support for several additional libraries for our usage. More than 100 supportive libraries are available for Processing. Let's take a glimpse at important library options in Processing.

From the IDE, click Sketch, then select Import Library and Add Library as shown in Figure 5-40.

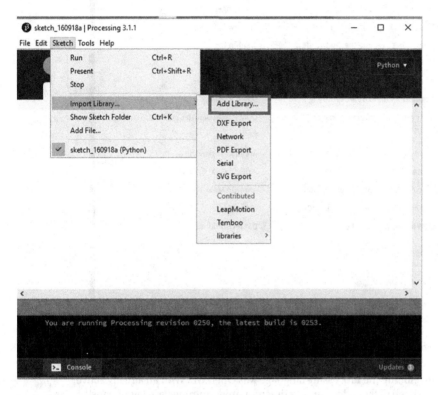

Figure 5-40. *Adding a library to the Processing IDE*

Figure 5-41 shows the library options available from the Processing IDE.

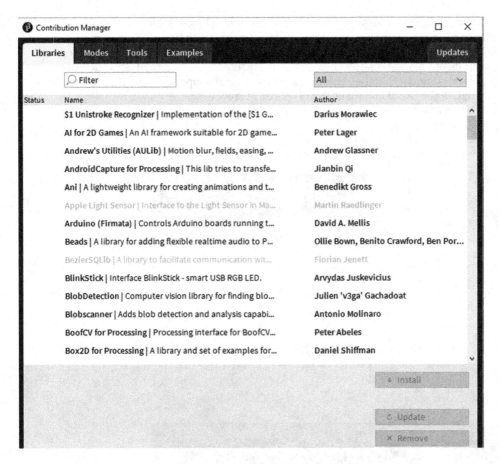

Figure 5-41. *Libraries available in the Processing IDE*

The inspiration for developing the Processing language was Open GL. With an already active community, Processing has been extended to support different programming language extensions, as depicted in Figure 5-42.

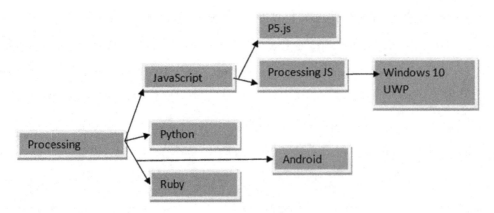

Figure 5-42. *Extended language support for Processing*

The structure of a processing app is represented in Figure 5-43.

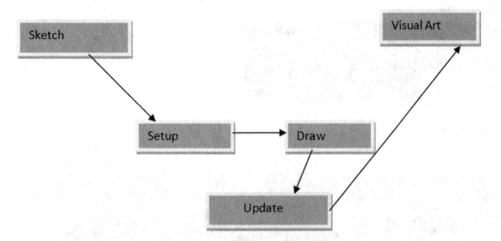

Figure 5-43. *The programming structure for Processing*

When you start working on a Processing project, two functions are particularly important. These functions are setup (), where you declare the size of the screen window, and the draw () function, with which we render the output.

Let's take a look at an example in Listing 5-3. We will draw an ellipse and as the mouse is pressed it will just move around.

Listing 5-3. Simple Processing Example

```
void setup() {
  size(1024, 768);
  noSmooth();
  fill(126);
  background(102);
}

void draw() {
  if (mousePressed) {
    stroke(255);
  } else {
    stroke(0);
  }
  ellipse(mouseX-30, mouseY, mouseX+30, mouseY);
  ellipse(mouseX, mouseY-30, mouseX, mouseY+30);
}
```

You need to click the Run button in the IDE, highlighted in Figure 5-44, to view the output, which is shown in Figure 5-45.

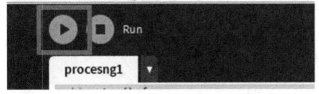

Figure 5-44. *Running the program*

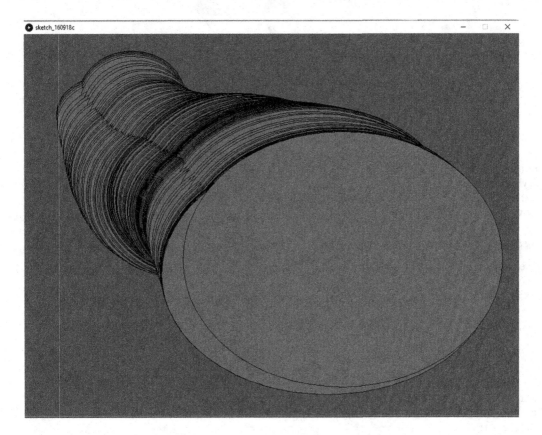

Figure 5-45. *The output*

Next we look at extending the Processing IDE for an Android extension. From the drop-down list at the right side of the IDE, select the Android option for adding a mode (see Figure 5-46).

Figure 5-46. *Add an Android mode*

The next option you see, shown in Figure 5-47, is for downloading the Android SDK (if it is not present) or setting it up manually.

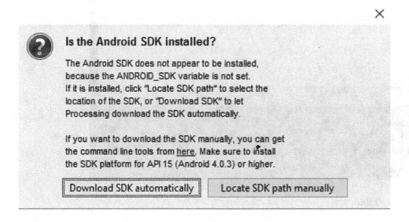

Figure 5-47. *Preparing the Android SDK*

If you click Download SDK Automatically, it will start the process. You can monitor the download progress in the dialog box shown in Figure 5-48.

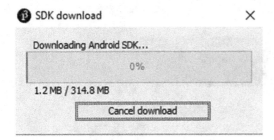

Figure 5-48. Downloading the Android SDK

Once the download is complete, the SDK is set up for Android on Processing (see Figure 5-49), so you can compile the app for Android.

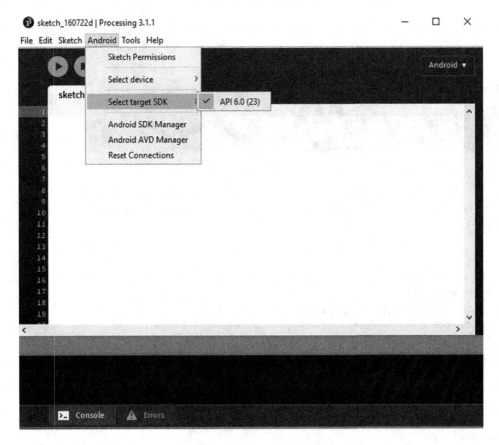

Figure 5-49. Android option is available

Summary

This chapter has covered creative coding and then gave an introduction to creative coding frameworks, in addition to an introduction to Processing.

CHAPTER 6

■ ■ ■

Extending Processing for UWP and IoT with Temboo

In Chapter 5 we went through working with creative coding and started with Processing. In this chapter, we show how Processing can be extended for the Universal Windows Platform and the Internet of Things (IoT) with Temboo platform.

Extending Processing

This chapter starts with a brief introduction to UWP. Then we provide a brief introduction to Processing JS and how to obtain it, followed by the procedure to build Processing JS UWP apps. We give examples and then build it as a package for store. Finally, we cover Processing in terms of IoT with Temboo.

UWP

The Windows 10 UWP platform is an architecture that is specifically designed for coding once it is deployed anywhere for Windows 10 device families. UWP apps run on all devices that run the Windows 10 OS, ranging from phones and tablets to PCs. The apps are generally built with the Visual Studio 2015 IDE. UWP is special because it is built in terms of a single API across all devices.

Figure 6-1 shows how UWP fits into a code once, deploy anywhere usage model.

© Abhishek Nandy and Debashree Chanda 2016

A. Nandy and D. Chanda, *Beginning Platino Game Engine*, DOI 10.1007/978-1-4842-2484-7_6

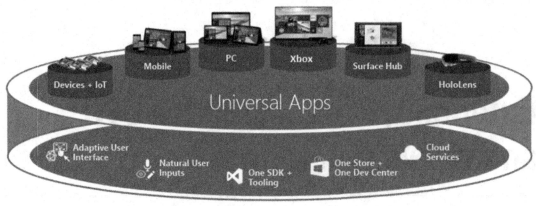

Figure 6-1. *Windows 10 UWP platform*

The Windows Store experience has also changed. It used to be different stores for different platforms, meaning different stores for mobile apps and Windows Store apps. Now it is one place where all the apps for the devices can be seen on the Dashboard and the option for monetization is also seen in a common place. Compatibilty has also changed, as now we can target different versions of Windows 10 the same as Android. This is called binary compatibility across all versions and all device families.

The speciality of UWP is that it can call all APIs across WinRT and also Win32 and .Net APIs, as depicted in Figure 6-2.

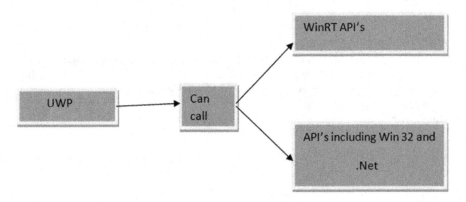

Figure 6-2. *UWP's capability*

Having one core API results in seamless API layer access for all devices. When we develop apps in Microsoft Visual Studio 2015, the result is a single app package that can be installed onto a wide range of devices. An adaptive UI and new features of the layout control help us to distribute a cool-looking app consumed in same manner across all devices.

Device Families

We know in the past, Windows 8 and Windows 8.1 used to target builds that were meant for either Windows Store or mobile devices. Now in Windows 10, though, we build apps and target them for different families that run Windows 10. When targeting an app, it is up to us to target which device we want to build it for.

Figure 6-3 shows that a child device inherits properties of the parent device and also its own functionality to the API, so this is an added combination that is felt across all devices on the platform.

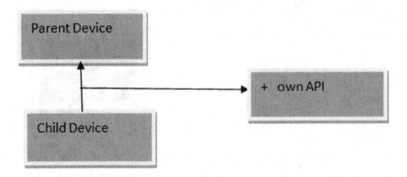

Figure 6-3. *Parent–child accessibilty UWP*

Consequence of Device Family Choice

As we choose from available platforms, say we are developing an app for IoT. We see that the app works perfectly if we install it on a Windows 10 IoT device, say Raspberry Pi3, and the host OS within the Pi3 device is Windows 10 IoT core. Being a minified version of the core, Windows 10 OS works hassle free. Because the development environment is the same, Visual Studio 2015, we can deploy the app to other sets of devices, too. Our idea when we develop an app should be to keep requirements minimal so that it can be deployed across all platforms. Restricting API access or including different functionality will not allow the app to work freely across different devices.

Making a Simple Hello World App with Visual Studio 2015

First, open Visual Studio 2015. Click File, then select New Project, Templates, JavaScript, Windows, Universal, and WinJS. Name the project app1, as shown in Figure 6-4. Click OK to continue.

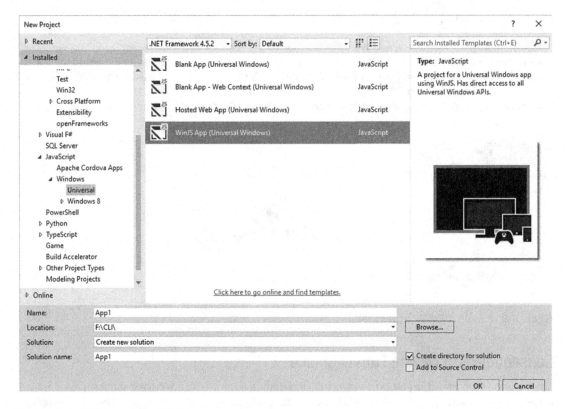

Figure 6-4. *UWP app using WinJS*

The next option we have is for targeting Windows 10 versions, as shown in Figure 6-5. Select a different version or keep this setting as it is, and then click OK.

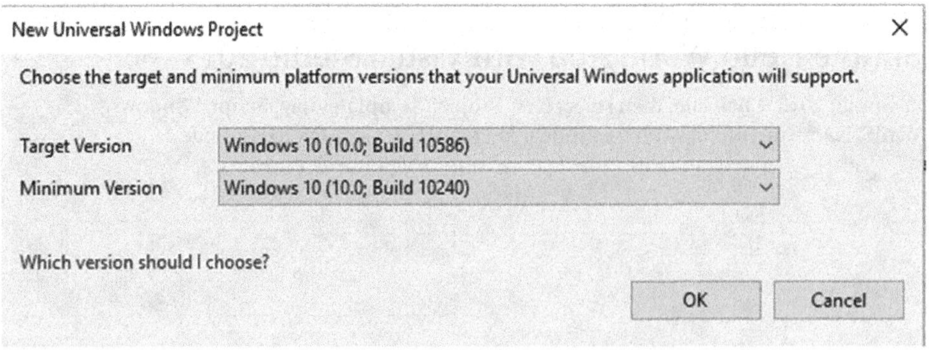

Figure 6-5. *Targeting the version of Windows 10*

Let's take a look at the file structure of the project in Figure 6-6.

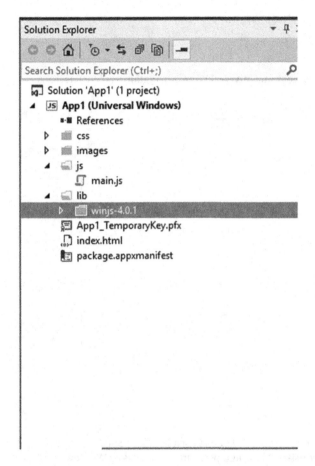

Figure 6-6. *The file structure for the project*

The most important file shown is the `main.js` file, which handles all the logic for Windows 10 activities. Together with the WinJS file, this file also binds the project. Within the `index.html` page, we include a Hello World within the body tag. Listing 6-1 shows the code part at `index.html`. This is the main page where we include JavaScript libraries.

Listing 6-1. The Coding Construct `index.html` Page

```
<!DOCTYPE html>
<html>
<head>
    <meta charset="utf-8" />
    <title>App1</title>
    <link href="lib/winjs-4.0.1/css/ui-light.css" rel="stylesheet" />
    <script src="lib/winjs-4.0.1/js/base.js"></script>
    <script src="lib/winjs-4.0.1/js/ui.js"></script>
    <link href="css/default.css" rel="stylesheet" />
    <script src="js/main.js"></script>
</head>
<body class="win-type-body">
```

```
    <div>HELLO WORLD!!</div>
</body>
</html>
```

Figure 6-7 shows the output when you run the program.Universal Windows Platform (UWP):devices:

Figure 6-7. *The output for the program*

WinJS

WinJS is an open source JavaScript library that helps us to build HTML5, Cascading Style Sheet (CSS), and JavaScript applications for Windows Store with a consistent look and performance across all Windows devices. It's a boon for Windows 10 to use one API across all devices. The flow of WinJS is shown in Figure 6-8.

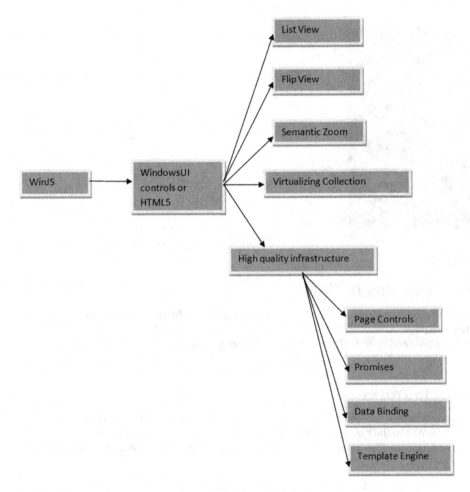

Figure 6-8. *WinJS flow*

Processing JS

As the name suggests, Processing JS (Figure 6-9) is a JavaScript port of the Processing language. With the booming web development scenario it is expected that it could be extended to HTML5 and JavaScript. It has the same ability to represent visual art forms in terms of coding with the additional capability of JavaScript bundled with the language support. The logic works this way: We write code in the Processing language, include it in a web page, and Processing JS performs the transformation, giving us the output.

Figure 6-9. *Processing JS*

Including the Processing JS library

We can target the development scenario in the index.html page when we add the Processing JS file to the header section of the web page.

Within the body tag, we need to add reference to the Processing (*.pde) script within the canvas tag and adddata-processing sources' attributes.

How Processing JS Works

When the extension was created, it was essential to know how the parsing happens from Processing language to Processing JS. Within the canvas, Processing scans the document with the data-processing sources' attributes, downloads the files using XMLHTTP Request, and finally turns it to the best usage as per JavaScript (see Figure 6-10).

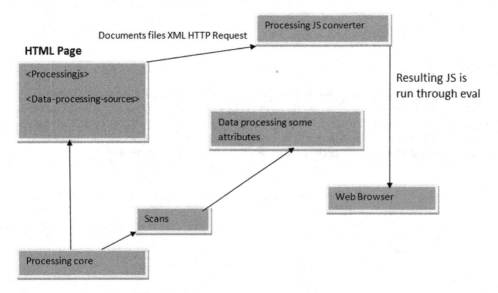

Figure 6-10. *Processing JS working structure*

Processing JS and Windows 10 UWP

This is the most important part of this chapter, where we include the concepts of creative coding and Processing JS and bring them to Windows 10 UWP apps. Now that you have grasped the concept of core Processing with respect to JavaScript, we can extend it to build Windows 10 UWP apps. Let's start.

Open Visual Studio 2015, then click File and select New Project. Create a Windows 10 UWP project that is WinJS based (see Figure 6-11).

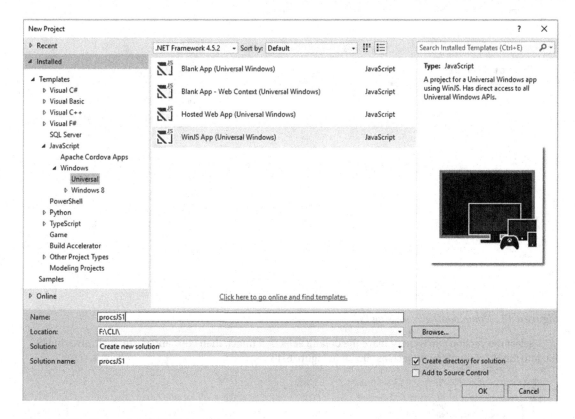

Figure 6-11. *Processing JS UWP app creation*

Next you need to download the Processing JS file and then include it in the project (see Figure 6-12).

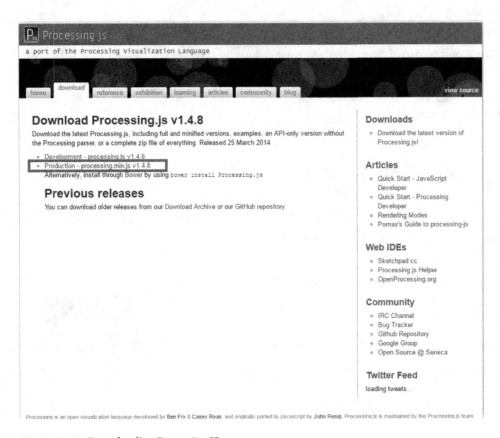

Figure 6-12. *Downloading Processing JS*

Select the version you want or leave the default selection intact, then copy and paste the Processing JS file into the JS folder of the project, as shown in Figure 6-13.

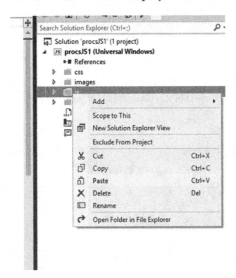

Figure 6-13. *Copy and paste the Processing JS file*

Next, create a folder, as demonstrated in Figure 6-14. Name the folder PDE and store the Processing file.

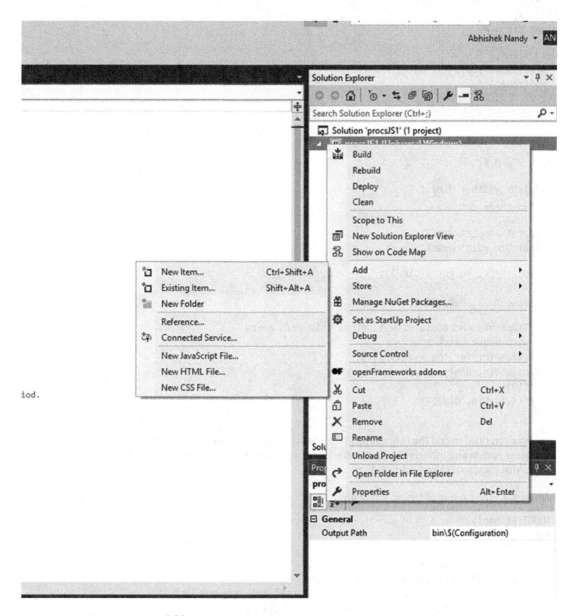

Figure 6-14. *Creating a new folder*

Next, start coding for the pde file. Let's try some simple code. The Processing code in Listing 6-2 allows a circle and a rectangle to move by mouse click.

Listing 6-2. Code for the Processing File

```
float x, y;
float dim = 80.0;

void setup() {
  size(1024, 768);
  noStroke();
}

void draw() {
  background(102);

  x = x + 0.8;

  if (x > width + dim) {
    x = -dim;
  }
  float X =mouseX-dim/2;
  float Dim =dim*mouseX;

  translate(x, height/2-dim/2);
  fill(255);
  ellipse(X, X, Dim, Dim);

  // Transforms accumulate. Notice how this rect moves
  // with mouse click
  // parameter for the x-axis value
  translate(x, dim);
  fill(0);
  rect(X,X, Dim, Dim);
}
```

Now you need to add the Processing JS file within the index.html page and then add the data-processing option and include the path to the folder where the Processing file is kept. The code inside the index.html page looks like Listing 6-3.

Listing 6-3. The Coding at index.html Page

```
<!DOCTYPE html>
<html>
<head>
    <meta charset="utf-8" />
    <title>procsJS1</title>
    <link href="lib/winjs-4.0.1/css/ui-light.css" rel="stylesheet" />
    <script src="lib/winjs-4.0.1/js/base.js"></script>
    <script src="lib/winjs-4.0.1/js/ui.js"></script>
    <link href="css/default.css" rel="stylesheet" />
    <script src="js/main.js"></script>
    <script src="js/processing.min.js"></script>
</head>
<body class="win-type-body">
    <canvas id="sketch" data-processing-sources="pde/move.pde"></canvas>
</body>
</html>
```

Let's run the app now. Figure 6-15 shows the app as it runs.

Figure 6-15. *The app runs and works well*

A Painting Processing JS App

We next create a painting app that works with mouse movements; that is, we will be using mouseX (Processing tracks mouse movements when the mouse cursor is across the screen area). We name the app ProcessingJS2. The steps performed for creating the project remain the same as those we have followed before.

The code for drawing the pattern is shown in Listing 6-4. It uses mouseX, mouseY, pmouseX, and pmouseY to draw lines.

Listing 6-4. The Code for the Drawing App

```
float d, dt;
void setup() {
  background (240,240,240);
  size(1000, 800);
  smooth();
  strokeWeight(0);
}
void draw() {
  d=dist( mouseX, mouseY, pmouseX, pmouseY);
  dt=map(sin(d),-1,1, 2, 4);
  print(dt);
```

```
if(mousePressed==true){
  stroke(180,0,0,180);
  strokeWeight(4+dt/2);
 line(mouseX, mouseY, pmouseX, pmouseY);

 stroke(90,90,0,180);
 strokeWeight((4+dt/2)/2);
line(mouseX+(4+dt/2)/2, mouseY-(4+dt/2)/2, pmouseX+(4+dt/2)/2, pmouseY-(4+dt/2)/2);

 stroke(0,180,0,180);
 strokeWeight(4+dt/2);
line(mouseX+(4+dt/2), mouseY-(4+dt/2), pmouseX+(4+dt/2), pmouseY-(4+dt/2));

stroke(0,90,90,180);
strokeWeight((4+dt/2)/2);
line(mouseX-(4+dt/2)/2, mouseY+(4+dt/2)/2, pmouseX-(4+dt/2)/2, pmouseY+(4+dt/2)/2);

stroke(0,0,180,180);
strokeWeight(4+dt/2);
line(mouseX-(4+dt/2), mouseY+(4+dt/2), pmouseX-(4+dt/2), pmouseY+(4+dt/2));

  }

}
```

When you run the app, the output will look something like Figure 6-16.

Figure 6-16. *Running the app to allow drawing*

Let's create an app package for the application you just created to validate that the Processing JS app runs perfectly and creates a successful Windows 10 UWP package.

Click Project, then select Store and click Create App Packages, as highlighted in Figure 6-17.

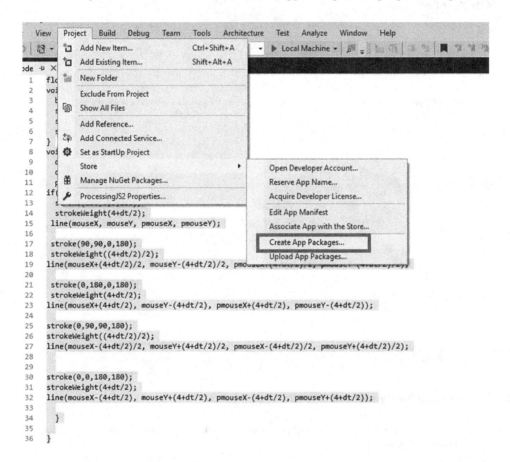

Figure 6-17. *Creating a package for the app*

The Create App Package Wizard opens. You will not push the app to the Windows Store, so select No, and then click Next, as shown in Figure 6-18.

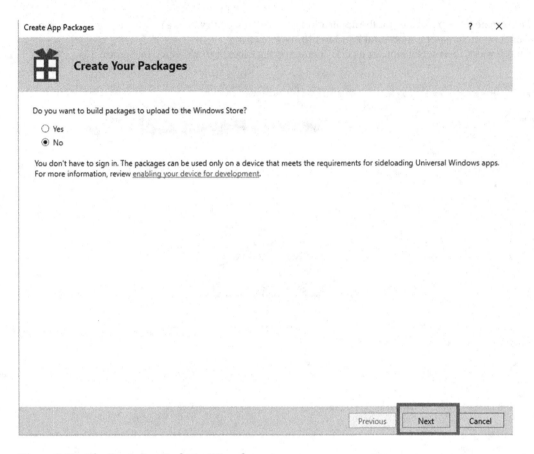

Figure 6-18. *The Create App Packages Wizard*

The next wizard page gives you the option to configure the app package. Leave the settings as shown, and click Create, as shown in Figure 6-19.

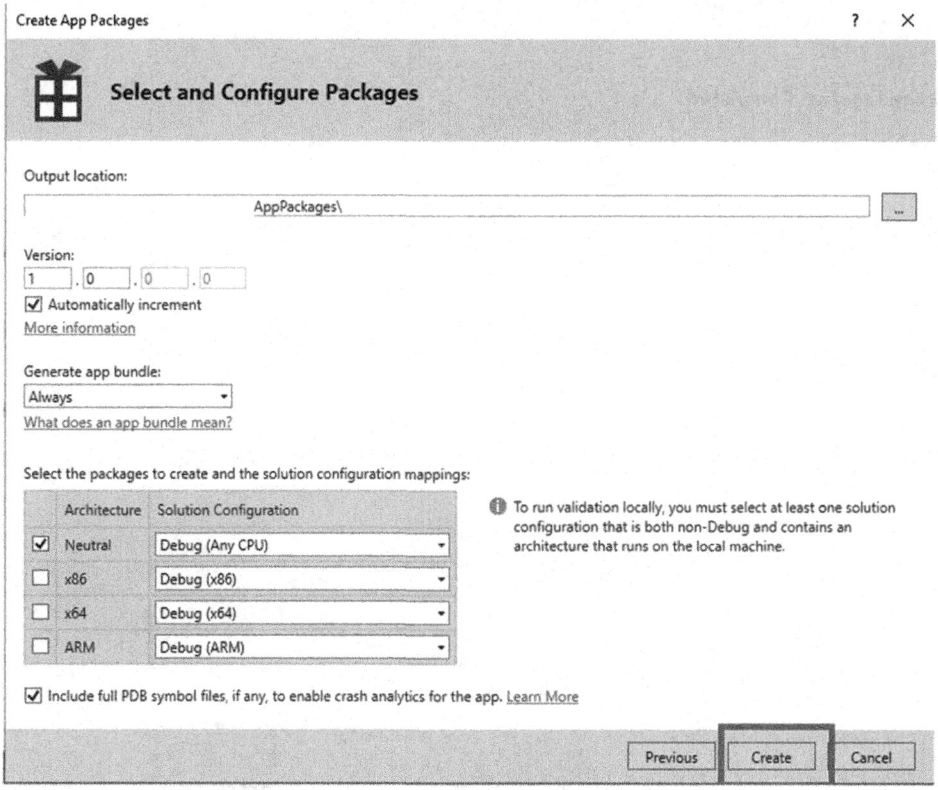

Figure 6-19. *Configuring and creating an app package*

On the final page of the wizard, shown in Figure 6-20, you can see that the app package has been created.

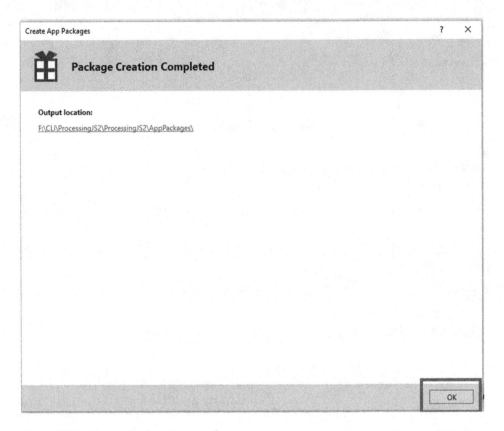

Figure 6-20. *The app package is created*

The experiment with Processing JS and Windows 10 UWP has succeeded and you are ready to create more apps for the Windows Store. You can take our imagination soaring and create creative coding apps for the store.

P5.js

P5.js (Figure 6-21) is a pure JavaScript version of the Processing language, so we don't have use any different technique to get the code going. We write the code for Processing in JavaScript.

🔒 https://p5js.org

p5.js Processing.py Processing for Android

p5*js

Download * Start * Reference * Libraries * Learn * Contribute

Hello! p5.js is a JavaScript library that starts with the original goal of
Processing, to make coding accessible for artists, designers, educators, and
beginners, and reinterprets this for today's web.

Using the original metaphor of a software sketchbook, p5.js has a full set
of drawing functionality. However, you're not limited to your drawing
canvas, you can think of your whole browser page as your sketch! For
this, p5.js has addon libraries that make it easy to interact with other
HTML5 objects, including text, input, video, webcam, and sound.

p5.js is a new interpretation, not an emulation or port, and it is in active
development. An official editing environment is coming soon, as well as
many more features!

p5.js was created by Lauren McCarthy and is developed by a community of collaborators, with support from the
Processing Foundation and NYU ITP. © Info.

Figure 6-21. *The P5.js web site*

First we need to download the P5.js library that we need to include in the project. The details of the
download page are shown in Figure 6-22.

p5*js

Processing fun times JavaScript quirkiness

Home

Download

Download

Gallery

Get Started

Reference

p5.js is open source, free software. All donations fund the Processing
Foundation, a nonprofit organization devoted to advancing the role of
programming within the visual arts through developing p5.js.
Donate here.

Libraries

Complete Library

Tutorials

Examples

p5.js complete
★
Includes:
p5.js, p5.dom.js, p5.sound.js, and an example project
Version 0.5.3 (August 17, 2016)

Books

Community

Contribute

Single Files

Forum

Github

Twitter

p5.js	p5.min.js	CDN
Single file:	Single file:	Link:
Full uncompressed version.	Compressed version.	Statically hosted file.

Editor

Figure 6-22. *Downloading the p5.js complete library*

Open a new project in Visual Studio 2015. Select the UWP and then the WinJS template, as we have done before. The result is shown in Figure 6-23.

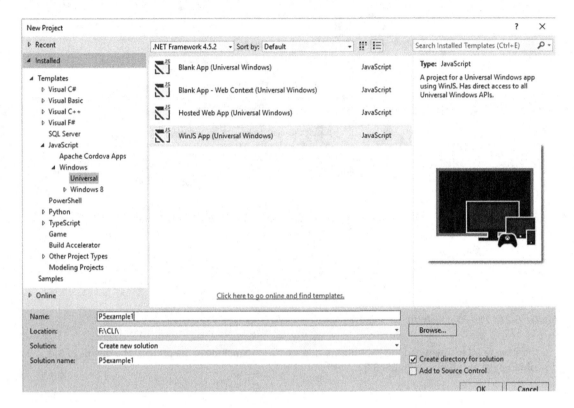

Figure 6-23. *Creating a UWP app*

Keep the platform version as it is, the way we have done before, and then click OK, as highlighted in Figure 6-24.

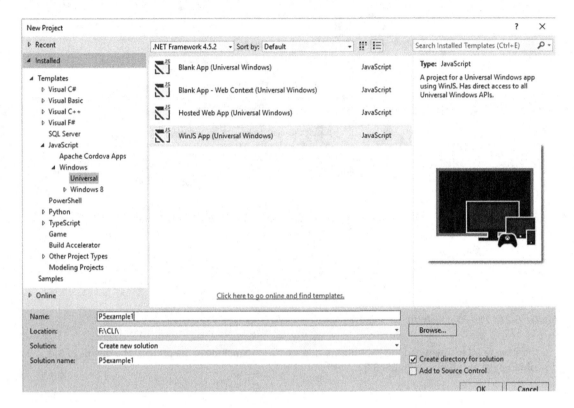

Figure 6-24. *Click OK for new project*

You need to copy the p5.js file to the JS folder, as shown in Figure 6-25. Once the file is copied, it helps in implementing Processing logic.

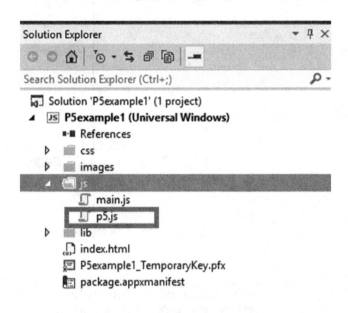

Figure 6-25. *The p5.js file in the JS folder*

Now you have to include the p5.js file within the index.html page. Create one JS file, as depicted in Figure 6-26, where we will be writing the code logic to get going with Processing.

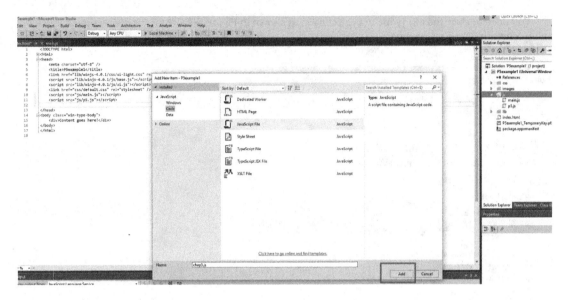

Figure 6-26. *Adding the JS file*

The functions are the same: We have the setup() and draw() functions, which we have used in Processing. Hence, we see that the entire logic resembles that of Processing. Let's take a look at the code in Listing 6-5, which allows us to interact with the balls that appear close to the rectangle with the mouse. We have used mouseX, mouseY utility of Processing all in core JavaScript.

Listing 6-5. The Code Logic in JS for Processing.

```
var angle1 = 0;
var angle2 = 0;
var scalar = 70;

function setup() {
    createCanvas(1920, 1080);
    noStroke();
    rectMode(CENTER);
}

function draw() {
    background(0);

    var ang1 = radians(angle1);
    var ang2 = radians(angle2);

    var x1 = mouseX + width / 2 + (scalar * cos(ang1));
    var x2 = pmouseX + width / 2 + (scalar * cos(ang2));
```

```
    var y1 = mouseY + height / 2 + (scalar * sin(ang1));
    var y2 = pmouseY + height / 2 + (scalar * sin(ang2));

    fill(255);
    rect(width * 0.5, height * 0.5, 140, 140);

    fill(0, 502, 553);
    ellipse(x1, height * 0.5 - 120, scalar, scalar);
    ellipse(x2, height * 0.5 + 120, scalar, scalar);

    fill(655, 604, 0);
    ellipse(width * 0.5 - 120, y1, scalar, scalar);
    ellipse(width * 0.5 + 120, y2, scalar, scalar);

    angle1 += 2;
    angle2 += 3;
}
```

The index.html file after adding chap5.js looks like Listing 6-6.

Listing 6-6. The index.html Page

```
<!DOCTYPE html>
<html>
<head>
    <meta charset="utf-8" />
    <title>P5example1</title>
    <link href="lib/winjs-4.0.1/css/ui-light.css" rel="stylesheet" />
    <script src="lib/winjs-4.0.1/js/base.js"></script>
    <script src="lib/winjs-4.0.1/js/ui.js"></script>
    <link href="css/default.css" rel="stylesheet" />
    <script src="js/main.js"></script>
    <script src="js/p5.js"></script>

</head>
<body class="win-type-body">

    <script src="js/chap5.js"></script>
</body>
</html>
```

When you run the app, the output should look like Figure 6-27.

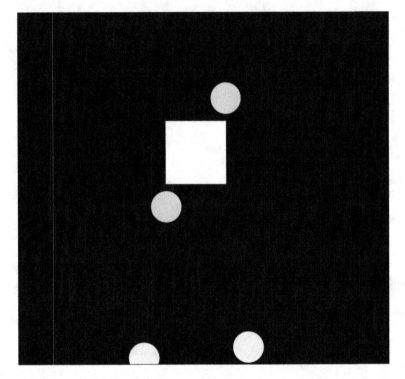

Figure 6-27. *The p5.js app running in Windows 10 UWP Platform*

After these experiments, you can see that Processing can be extended easily to Windows 10 UWP with Processing JS, as well as P5.js, so we have covered a new area in terms of creative coding and Windows 10 UWP. Next we discuss IoT briefly and then extend Processing for IoT with Temboo.

IoT

Any device that has a capability to acquire an IP address can be considered an IoT device. If we have a network where we are connected across numerous devices communicating, sharing information, and working with responses from each other we can say the network has implemented IoT. IoT devices share information via cloud and currently service providers such as Windows Azure, IBM Bluemix, and AWS all offer a different IoT suite for use across these devices.

There are some special boards for usage across different platforms, such as Intel Edison, Intel Joule, Raspberry Pi2, and Raspberry Pi3.

There is a catch with operating systems in these devices, too. The OS is a minified version of the core OS we use in the everyday laptops and PCs that we are using. For Linux, for example, we have Yocto Linux, which is a minified version of the core Linux distribution. The same is true with other Linux kernels, too. For Windows we have a minified version of Windows 10 OS called Windows 10 IoT core.

Security on an IoT device is implemented via IoT gateways, which store or allow communication between different IoT devices while checking the information flow gathered in the IoT gateway and analyzing the headers.

The IoT devices are connected to different sensors to collect data and share across the connected IoT network and also to help in visualizing the data.

Processing IoT and Temboo

Temboo

Temboo is a platform to easily integrate IoT devices and the sensor data across the Web with very simple logic. The Temboo application on the Web looks like Figure 6-28.

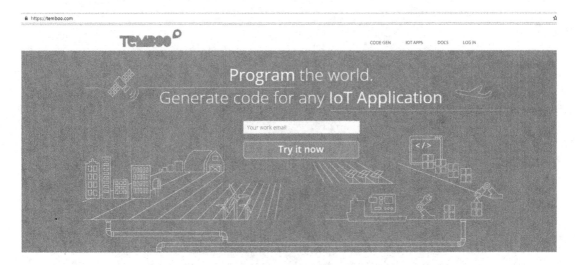

Figure 6-28. Temboo platform

Perfect

You will need to enter a user ID and password to log in; otherwise, you will need to create an account.

When you log in, you have the option of choosing from where to learn. For this exercise, choose Processing, as highlighted in Figure 6-29.

LEARN

Figure 6-29. Processing option chosen

You will then see that the Processing option is enabled in Temboo, as shown in Figure 6-30.

LEARN
P
Processing
Get Started with the Processing SDK
Examples & Tutorials for Temboo & Processing
Explore pre-built IoT Applications

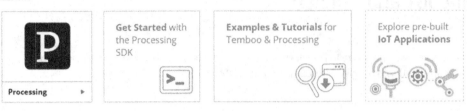

Figure 6-30. *Processing option enabled*

If you click Get Started With Processing, it will suggest that you download the library and save it to the Processing location, as depicted in Figure 6-31.

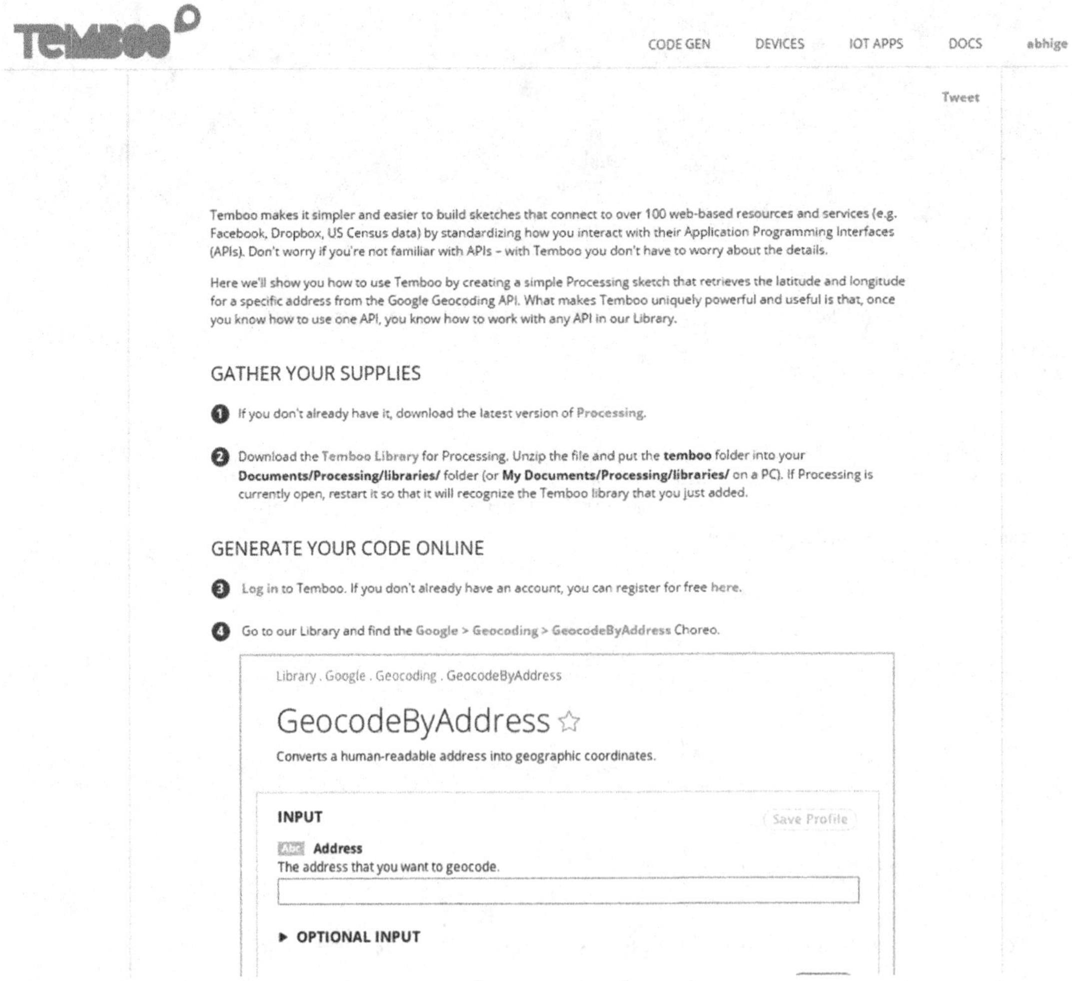

CODE GEN
DEVICES
IOT APPS
DOCS
abhige
Tweet
Temboo makes it simpler and easier to build sketches that connect to over 100 web-based resources and services (e.g. Facebook, Dropbox, US Census data) by standardizing how you interact with their Application Programming Interfaces (APIs). Don't worry if you're not familiar with APIs - with Temboo you don't have to worry about the details.
Here we'll show you how to use Temboo by creating a simple Processing sketch that retrieves the latitude and longitude for a specific address from the Google Geocoding API. What makes Temboo uniquely powerful and useful is that, once you know how to use one API, you know how to work with any API in our Library.
GATHER YOUR SUPPLIES
1 If you don't already have it, download the latest version of Processing.
2 Download the Temboo Library for Processing. Unzip the file and put the temboo folder into your Documents/Processing/libraries/ folder (or My Documents/Processing/libraries/ on a PC). If Processing is currently open, restart it so that it will recognize the Temboo library that you just added.
GENERATE YOUR CODE ONLINE
3 Log in to Temboo. If you don't already have an account, you can register for free here.
4 Go to our Library and find the Google > Geocoding > GeocodeByAddress Choreo.
Library . Google . Geocoding . GeocodeByAddress
GeocodeByAddress
Converts a human-readable address into geographic coordinates.
INPUT
Save Profile
Abc Address
The address that you want to geocode.
▸ OPTIONAL INPUT

Figure 6-31. *How to start Temboo with Processing*

Every possible thing in Temboo is done through Choreo, so let's see how that looks. Make sure you have downloaded the library files for Processing and copied them to the correct path. We will be using Envirosearch Choreo, and start with finding the zip code for Los Angeles, as shown in Figure 6-32.

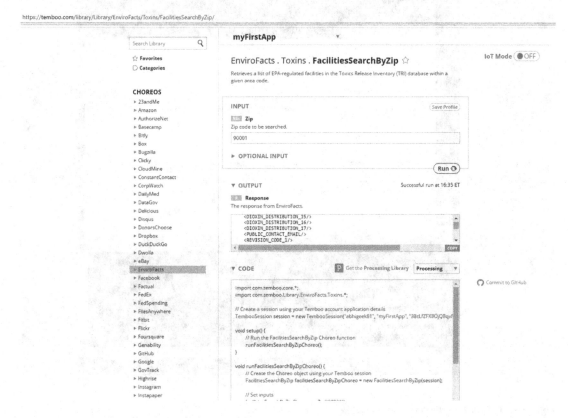

Figure 6-32. *Temboo EnviroFacts Choreo*

Let's run the code in Processing. We see the output shown in Figure 6-33. Name the app FirstChoreo.

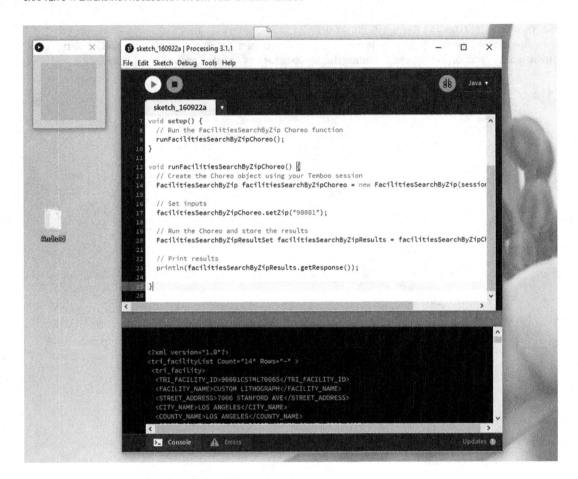

Figure 6-33. *Running the code in Processing*

The code is given in Listing 6-7.

Listing 6-7. The Code for Processing with Temboo

```
import com.temboo.core.*;
import com.temboo.Library.EnviroFacts.Toxins.*;

// Create a session using your Temboo account application details
TembooSession session = new TembooSession("abhigeek81", "myFirstApp",
"38cLfZFX8OjQ8qvMW1wiktIE6msnvQv2");

void setup() {
  // Run the FacilitiesSearchByZip Choreo function
  runFacilitiesSearchByZipChoreo();
}

void runFacilitiesSearchByZipChoreo() {
  // Create the Choreo object using your Temboo session
  FacilitiesSearchByZip facilitiesSearchByZipChoreo = new FacilitiesSearchByZip(session);
```

```
// Set inputs
facilitiesSearchByZipChoreo.setZip("90001");

// Run the Choreo and store the results
FacilitiesSearchByZipResultSet facilitiesSearchByZipResults = facilitiesSearchByZipChoreo.
run();

// Print results
println(facilitiesSearchByZipResults.getResponse());

}Internet of Things (IoT)and TembooCode for Processing
```

Next, use the DailyMed Choreo. First use SearchByName for drug details, as depicted in Figure 6-34.

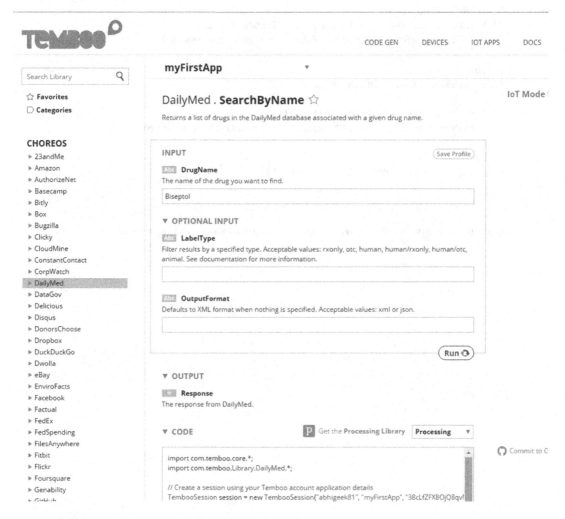

Figure 6-34. *Searching on a drug name*

The code for this is given in Listing 6-8.

Listing 6-8. The Code for Finding the Drug Detail

```
import com.temboo.core.*;
import com.temboo.Library.DailyMed.*;

// Create a session using your Temboo account application details
TembooSession session = new TembooSession("abhigeek81", "myFirstApp",
"38cLfZFX8OjQ8qvMW1wiktIE6msnvQv2");

void setup() {
        // Run the SearchByName Choreo function
        runSearchByNameChoreo();
}

void runSearchByNameChoreo() {
        // Create the Choreo object using your Temboo session
        SearchByName searchByNameChoreo = new SearchByName(session);

        // Set inputs
        searchByNameChoreo.setDrugName("Biseptol");

        // Run the Choreo and store the results
        SearchByNameResultSet searchByNameResults = searchByNameChoreo.run();

        // Print results
        println(searchByNameResults.getResponse());

}
```

When you run the code in Processing, you will get the output shown in Figure 6-35.

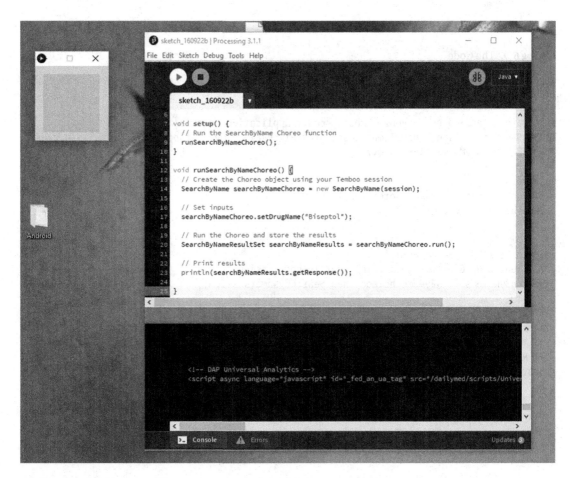

Figure 6-35. *The output runs*

The code for the output is shown in Listing 6-9.

Listing 6-9. The Code

```
import com.temboo.core.*;
import com.temboo.Library.DailyMed.*;

// Create a session using your Temboo account application details
TembooSession session = new TembooSession("abhigeek81", "myFirstApp",
"38cLfZFX8OjQ8qvMW1wiktIE6msnvQv2");

void setup() {
  // Run the SearchByName Choreo function
  runSearchByNameChoreo();
}

void runSearchByNameChoreo() {
  // Create the Choreo object using your Temboo session
  SearchByName searchByNameChoreo = new SearchByName(session);

  // Set inputs
  searchByNameChoreo.setDrugName("Biseptol");

  // Run the Choreo and store the results
  SearchByNameResultSet searchByNameResults = searchByNameChoreo.run();

  // Print results
  println(searchByNameResults.getResponse());

}
```

Summary

In this chapter we integrated Processing into Windows 10 UWP and then also extended Processing for Temboo. The book thus concluded with some simple constructs of creative coding in a different way.

Index

© Abhishek Nandy and Debashree Chanda 2016
A. Nandy and D. Chanda, *Beginning Platino Game Engine*, DOI 10.1007/978-1-4842-2484-7

Get the eBook for only $4.99!

Why limit yourself?

Now you can take the weightless companion with you wherever you go and access your content on your PC, phone, tablet, or reader.

Since you've purchased this print book, we are happy to offer you the eBook for just $4.99.

Convenient and fully searchable, the PDF version enables you to easily find and copy code—or perform examples by quickly toggling between instructions and applications.

To learn more, go to http://www.apress.com/us/shop/companion or contact support@apress.com.

Printed in the United States
By Bookmasters